Lecture Notes in Artificial Intelligence   10237

Subseries of Lecture Notes in Computer Science

More information about this series at http://www.springer.com/series/1244

Adrian David Cheok · Kate Devlin
David Levy (Eds.)

Love and Sex with Robots

Second International Conference, LSR 2016
London, UK, December 19–20, 2016
Revised Selected Papers

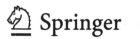 Springer

Editors
Adrian David Cheok
Imagineering Institute
Iskandar Puteri
Malaysia

and

City, University of London
London
UK

Kate Devlin
Goldsmiths, University of London
London
UK

David Levy
Intelligent Toys Ltd.
London
UK

ISSN 0302-9743   ISSN 1611-3349   (electronic)
Lecture Notes in Artificial Intelligence
ISBN 978-3-319-57737-1   ISBN 978-3-319-57738-8   (eBook)
DOI 10.1007/978-3-319-57738-8

Library of Congress Control Number: 2017938166

LNCS Sublibrary: SL7 – Artificial Intelligence

Printed on acid-free paper

This Springer imprint is published by Springer Nature
The registered company is Springer International Publishing AG
The registered company address is: Gewerbestrasse 11, 6330 Cham, Switzerland

Preface

Intimate relationships, such as love and sex, between human and machines, especially robots, has been one of the main topics in science fiction. However, this topic has never been treated in the academic area until recently. The topic was first raised and discussed by David Levy in his book titled *Love and Sex with Robotics* published in 2007. The book found an eager public in North America who wanted to know more. During the period immediately prior to publication of the book and for a few months afterwards, the topic caught the imagination of the media, not just in the USA and Canada but on a worldwide scale. During those months David Levy gave around 120 interviews, by telephone, e-mail, and in person; to newspapers, magazines, radio, and TV stations and to electronic media. Television interviews included an appearance on The Colbert Report (2008); as well as visits to his home by TV crews from Russia, Canada, Austria, France, Germany, Switzerland, and other countries. There was also, not surprisingly, a flurry of interest from women's magazines, including *Elle* and *Marie Claire*. And the coverage in general science publications included articles in *IEEE Technology and Society Magazine, MIT Technology Review, Scientific American, and Wired*.

In the academic world there has already been sufficient coverage of the topic to demonstrate rather convincingly that it is of interest not only for mainstream media; an academically rewritten version of the book titled *Intimate Relationships with Artificial Partners* also attracted much media publicity. Conferences on robotics, AI, and other computer science-related subjects began to accept and even invite papers on the subject, and there have thus far been two conferences devoted specifically to human–robot personal relationships. In 2014 the First International Congress of Love and Sex with Robots was held in Madeira. The academic journals that have since chosen to publish papers on the topic have included: *Accountability in Research, AI & Society, Artificial Intelligence, Current Sociology, Ethics and Information Technology, Futures, Industrial Robot, International Journal of Advanced Robotic Systems, International Journal of Social Development, International Journal of Social Robotics, International Journal of Technoethics, New Media and Society, Phenomenology and the Cognitive Sciences, Philosophy Technology, Social Robotics, Technological Forecasting and Social Change*, and various publications from the IEEE, Springer, and other highly respected technology stables. One paper, from Victoria University of Wellington, New Zealand, achieved a high profile in the general media when it appeared in 2012 for its entertaining depiction of a future scenario in the red light district of Amsterdam – a life, in 2050, revolving around android prostitutes "who are clean of sexually transmitted infections (STIs), not smuggled in from Eastern Europe and forced into slavery, the city council will have direct control over android sex workers controlling prices, hours of operations and sexual services."

Since the initial burst of media interest late in 2007 there have also been TV documentaries and feature movies in which sex with robots, with virtual characters, or with life-sized sex dolls was the dominant theme: *Lars and the Real Girl, Meaning of*

Robots (which had its premiere at the 2012 Sundance Festival), *My Sex Robot, Her* (2013), and the BBC TV documentary *Guys and Dolls* as well as the 2004 remake of *The Stepford Wives*. This points out that it is the sexual nature of the subject matter which is responsible. Sex sells.

Following the storm of publicity by the launch of the David Levy's book in 2007, the subject of human–robot romantic and intimate relationships rapidly developed into an academic research discipline in its own right. The subject was named "lovotics," a term coined by Adrian David Cheok.

The interest in this field from the academic community resulted, in 2013, in the founding of a journal and e-journal devoted entirely to the subject, whose Editor-in-Chief is Adrian David Cheok. *Lovotics* (*Lovotics Journal*) defines its own domain as "academic studies of love and friendship with robots."

March 2017

Adrian David Cheok
Kate Devlin
David Levy
Kasun Karunanayaka

Organization

Organizing Committee

General Chairs

Adrian David Cheok   City, University of London, UK and Imagineering
Institute, Malaysia
Kate Devlin   Goldsmiths, University of London, UK
David Levy   Intelligent Toys Ltd., London, UK

Program Committee

Anton Nijholt
Yorick Wilks
Elisabeth Andre
Alexiei Dingli
Jaap van den Herik
Patrick Gebhard
Trudy Barber
Hidenobu Sumioka
Vic Grout
Cristina Portales
Emma Yann Zhang
Sumayya Ebrahim
Julie Wosk
Randy Goebel
Yuefang Zhou
Chamari Edirisinghe
Jessica Mitchell

Sponsor

Media Partner

*Multimodal Technologies
and Interaction*

Contents

Keynote Talk

Why Not Marry a Robot?

David Levy[✉]

Retro Computers Ltd., London, UK
david@retro-computers.co.uk

Abstract. The trend of robotics research and development, from industrial robots to service robots to companion and carer robots, has as its logical continuation the design and construction of partner robots, sufficiently human-like and sufficiently appealing in various ways to take on the role of a partner in a relationship with a human being. This trend immediately raises many questions relating to humans loving and being loved by robots, treating robots as life partners and being similarly treated by them, marrying robots and having sex with robots. We discuss some aspects of human-robot marriage and reassess the author's 10-year-old prediction that the first human-robot marriage will take place in the state of Massachusetts around the year 2050.

1   Introduction

The trend of robotics research and development, from industrial robots to service robots to companion and carer robots for the elderly, has as its logical continuation the design and construction of partner robots, sufficiently human-like and sufficiently appealing in various ways to take on the role of a partner in a relationship with a human being. This logical continuation of the trend raises many questions relating to humans loving and being loved by robots, treating robots as life partners and being similarly treated by them, having sex with robots, and, ultimately, marrying robots.

Arthur Harkins, an anthropology professor at the University of Minnesota, caused astonishment in the mid-1970 s when he predicted that, before the year 2000, the first test case of a human-robot marriage would be in the courts. At that time, the media bombarded Harkins with requests for interviews, many of which were on TV talk-shows with a phone-in audience, and "... *as people called in, once they got over their initial shock, their next question was invariably consistent: 'Where do I get one?'*" Clearly Harkins' estimated timescale was wrong, but today his idea id very much on the robotics road map.

Ten years ago, at the EURON *Roboethics* Atelier in Genoa, Italy, I presented three papers [1–3], on some of the subject matter which the following year formed the backbone of my book *Love + Sex with Robots* [4]. To the best of my knowledge those talks were the first ever delivered to an academic conference on such a subject. They created only very tiny ripples in the ocean of academic research, but by the end of the following year *Love and Sex with Robots* had begun to be rather widely talked about. That was only partly due to the truth of the old adage "sex sells", more so to HarperCollins, the

© Springer International Publishing AG 2017
A.D. Cheok et al. (Eds.): LSR 2016, LNAI 10237, pp. 3–13, 2017.
DOI: 10.1007/978-3-319-57738-8_1

New York publisher of my book, who arranged some 120 media interviews for me, including a TV appearance on *the Colbert Report* in the USA which elevated the popularity of the topic to the mainstream. By then public interest in the topic had already spread to Europe, where my defence of my PhD thesis at the University of Maastricht [5] brought the university more publicity than any other in its history.

Consider what most people want from a life-partner, a spouse. All of the following qualities and many more are likely to be achievable in software within a few decades - your robot will be: patient, kind, protective, loving, trusting, truthful, persevering, respectful, uncomplaining, complimentary, pleasant to talk to, and sharing your sense of humour. And the robots of the future will not be jealous, boastful, arrogant, rude, self-seeking or easily angered, unless of course you want them to be.

So let us consider the possibility of marrying one.

2   Robot Personhood

Any discussion of marriage to a robot raises the question – what type of entity should we consider an intelligent robot to be? How should we categorize it? Robot personhood is steadily becoming a significant issue for lawmakers and those working in the field of social robotics. Before many years have passed, society will need to take some very important decisions as to whether intelligent robots should be regarded as persons or as some type of person, and if so, what should be their legal standing? What laws should apply to how we may treat them, and what laws will they need to obey? *"The legal rights of robots"* is a topic which has been debated now for more than 30 years, starting with a prescient 1985 paper by Robert Freitas Jnr with exactly that title [6]. The time is fast approaching when the theoretical debate must evolve into laws, and the consequences of those laws will be staggering.

One of the fundamental questions affecting whether or not marriages to robots should be legalized, is should robots be regarded, legally, as persons, or at least as some type of person? In recent years the subject of robot personhood has come to the fore in Social Robotics, with publication titles such as:

"The Electronic Agent: A Legal Personality Under German law" (2003) [7]

"A Legal Theory for Autonomous Artificial Agents" (2011) [8]

"Do Androids Dream? Personhood and Intelligent Artifacts" (2011) [9]

"Can Machines be People? Reflections on the Turing Triage Test" (2012) [10]

[Rob Sparrow's paper describes a test, proposed by him in 2004, to determine whether or not a machine has achieved the moral standing of people.]

"The Outline of Personhood Law Regarding Artificial Intelligences and Emulated Human Entities" (2014) [11]

"Machine Minds: Frontiers of Legal Personhood" (2015) [12]

It is already well established that entities such as corporations are treated as having a legal status, but it is as yet an open question whether the same will be true of intelligent robots. Clearly this is a question deserving serious consideration. Should we recognize robots and protect the will of a robot? In his essay *"Machine Minds"*, Evan Zimmerman supports the idea of granting such rights to robots, basing his argument on technical law and providing a justification for bestowing personhood. Zimmerman demonstrates that the development of personhood involves analyzing fully conscious entities and how such consciousnesses could be allowed to exercise their will. He argues that the basis for designing future intelligent machines is likely to be the workings of the human brain, and he makes a nod to the cyborg – a human-machine combination. A person with one artificial limb is still a person, as is someone with two, three or four artificial limbs. So a person does not lose their personhood for undergoing augmentation by a prosthetic, nor is a person with an artificial heart any less human as a result. So the question arises – would someone whose brain has undergone augmentation or partial replacement be any less human? And what about someone with a wholly artificial brain? Since a person does not lose their personhood just because they have one or more artificial parts, I argue that a robot does not necessarily lack personhood just because it is built differently from a human, nor is that difference alone sufficient reason to deny a robot the same rights and protections ascribed to humans.

Christophe Leroux and colleagues were given the responsibility by the European Robotics Coordinated Action Group to develop arguments on ethical, legal and social issues in robotics. Their report, published in 2012, is entitled *"Suggestions for a Green Paper on Legal Issues in Robotics"* [13]. Leroux et al. recommend that, for the time being, robots should not have the legal status of humans, rather they should be assigned to a specially established legal category to which Leroux et al. refer as "electronic personhood". They base this suggestion on the notion of a "legal person" such as a corporation, a company. Such entities are treated by the law in many of the same ways as are people, with similar capacities and financial responsibilities for example, though they are not endowed with the same legal status as humans in certain other respects. Leroux *et al.* explain:

> "A similar approach is plausible for at least some "autonomous" machines. Robots are neither humans nor animals but can develop a certain artificial personality, a certain scope of action, and a certain "tangible symbol" for the cooperation of all the people creating and using that specific robot... Jurisprudence could establish some autonomous machines as having the status

of an "electronic person" with specific rights and obligations. This would apply only to particular contexts, and would include autonomous machines having a certain degree of legal autonomy... If an electronic person causes an injury to a third person,... he can be sued directly... Some further questions yet to be answered are: When does the legal personhood start and end? Which rights and obligations come with it? What restrictions are useful?" [13]

Since 1927 *Time* magazine has awarded an annual accolade to recognize remarkable worldwide achievements. In 1982 their title "Man-of-the-Year" went to the personal computer, and legend has it that Steve Jobs cried when he learned that the title was not being awarded to him instead. More recently the title was renamed "Person-of-the-Year", and I speculate that before many more years have passed it will be awarded to the humanoid robot, such is their fast approaching encroachment and integration into society and their rapid acquisition of the characteristics and qualities usually associated with personhood.

It is by accepting the possibility of robots as being endowed with some sort of artificial personhood, that we can make it more palatable to consider how best to govern the intelligent robotic systems of the future. Regulations that allow robot companions to have a legal status similar to that of a corporation will pave the way for robot personhood, robot rights, and ultimately the possibility of human-robot marriage.

3   The Legal Evolution of Marriage

Restrictive laws affecting the institution of marriage have undergone a massive reinvention in the Western world since the middle of the 20th century. Until 1967 some American states still banned interracial marriage – the U.S. government's position on the matter was that each state had the right to decide for itself whether or not to permit marriage across the divide between Blacks and Whites. It was only following a Supreme Court decision in 1967 that interracial marriage in the USA was finally made fully legal in *all* U.S. states.

Even more controversial than the opposition to interracial marriage was and still is the issue of same sex marriage. With the late 20th century trend of wider acceptance for gay and lesbian relationships, it is hardly surprising that many same-sex couples strove for the right to marry their partners. The idea itself was hardly new – in Africa, for example, the Nuer and some other peoples have long favoured woman-woman marriages [14].

The gay rights movement which started in 1970 s America was primarily aimed at legalising homosexual and lesbian relationships – marriage was not a primary aim. But once same-sex relationships started to become legally recognized in the USA it was only a matter of time before the gay and lesbian communities demanded more, with the American movement gaining support from some of the free thinking European countries such as the Netherlands and Denmark – the latter becoming the first country to recognize what the Danes call "legally registered partnerships". On October 1st 1989 six homosexual couples were legally joined in such partnerships in a room in Copenhagen's City Hall, giving them, under Danish law, most of the rights of married heterosexuals, but not the right to adopt or obtain joint custody of a child [15].

The transition from having one's same-sex relationship legally recognized, to being able to enter into marriage with one's same-sex partner, came relatively quickly after the Copenhagen event. It was in the Netherlands, a land with healthily liberal attitudes to lifestyle choices, that the first legalized same-sex marriage took place in a Western country. The Dutch parliament had set up a special commission in 1995 to investigate the issue, and following the commission's recommendations a same-sex marriage law was passed by the Dutch House of Representatives and the Senate in the year 2000, coming into effect on April 1st 2001. Since then the Dutch innovation has been followed by similar laws in a number of other European countries, as well as Canada, South Africa, Argentina, Brazil, Uruguay, New Zealand and Columbia, and in 2015 by the United States, where President Obama, three years earlier, had become the first sitting US President to publicly declare his support for same-sex marriage to be legalized.

But President Obama was not always in favour – he had wavered back and forth before coming down firmly on the side of this form of social progress. By the end of 2010 he was supporting civil unions which gave partners rights that are equivalent to those of a husband and wife in a regular marriage, and he freely admitted that his attitude to same-sex marriage was evolving. In 2012 he said that he believed that same-sex couples should be allowed to marry but that it was up to each state to decide whether or not to support such marriages. By 2014 his opinion had evolved further – he decided that same-sex marriage should become legal in all fifty states.

At the other end of the political spectrum Newt Gingrich went through a similar evolution. In 2008 he had described same-sex marriage as showing *"an outrageous disrespect for our Constitution and for the majority of the people of the United States who believe marriage is the union of husband and wife"* [16]. But within 2 years Gingrich had come to accept civil same-sex marriages, though not religious ones, and he encouraged his party, the Republican Party, to accept that same-sex marriage was going to be legalized in more and more states as time went on.

During those years leading up to the American Supreme Court decision of 2015, which legalized same-sex marriage in every American state, public opinion moved in the same direction as Obama and Gingrich were moving. A poll taken by CNN in August 2010 revealed that 49% of those surveyed believed that gay and lesbian couples have a constitutional right to marry. By February 2015 that support had risen to 63%. Other polls conducted by Gallup and by the Washington Post show similar increases in support. The rapidity of this increase over a time span of just a few years demonstrates that nowadays public attitudes to such intimate matters can undergo rapid liberalizing change. This does not surprise me at all. During the past couple of years or so I have observed a steady increase in the frequency with which I am asked to give media interviews on the subject of robot sex and asked about robot marriage, and there has been a commensurate increase in the amount of media exposure for these subjects. This increase points to a near future in which robot sex will be a very hot topic, and with it will come an intensification of the debate on the subject of human-robot marriage.

4 For and Against Marriage to Robots

The controversy over same-sex marriage gives us a few clues as to some of the arguments likely to be adopted by those who debate the issue of marriage to a robot. In the USA the Defence of Marriage Act (DOMA) became a federal law in September 1996. Section 3 of the Act, which was often used to argue against same-sex marriage, espoused the following definition of marriage:

> *"In determining the meaning of any Act of Congress, or of any ruling, regulation, or interpre-tation of the various administrative bureaus and agencies of the United States, the word 'marriage' means only a legal union between one man and one woman as husband and wife, and the word 'spouse' refers only to a person of the opposite sex who is a husband or a wife."* [17]

This definition lasted in U.S. federal law for only 7 years, after which it was declared unconstitutional, and it was the abolishment of this definition which paved the way for the legalization, in all 50 American states, of same-sex marriage. But even though the DOMA definition is no longer law, the public sentiment behind it is still quite strong. I suspect that the majority of people who join the robot marriage debate will, for the next two or three decades, argue that a marriage can only be between two humans, and not between one human and a robot or some other non-human entity.

Religion is one reason for opposing same-sex marriage, but it is not at all clear that the same religious arguments will hold much water when applied to the concept of human-robot marriage. A typical opposition statement against same-sex marriage, founded on religious thinking, came from the Southern Baptist Convention, an American Christian denomination with more than 15 million members in the USA. In June 2003 the Convention adopted a statement confirming that:

> *"Legalizing same-sex "marriage" would convey a societal approval of a homosexual lifestyle, which the Bible calls sinful and dangerous both to the individuals involved and to society at large* [18].*"*

In support of this statement the Convention affirmed that:

> *"legal and biblical marriage can only occur between one man and one woman"*

But so far as I am aware, nowhere in the Bible does it say anything against other types of marriage. Nowhere does it say that a marriage must be between two humans.

Parenting is another contentious issue employed by those who argue against same-sex marriage. A common argument is that, in order to have a well balanced upbringing, children need both a male father and a female mother, but evidence from paediatrics experts runs counter to that argument. The American Academy of Pediatrics, for example, published an analysis in the journal *"Pediatrics"* in 2006, in which they stated:

> *"There is ample evidence to show that children raised by same-gender parents fare as well as those raised by heterosexual parents. More than 25 years of research have documented that there is no relationship between parents' sexual orientation and any measure of a child's emotional, psychosocial, and behavioral adjustment. These data have demonstrated no risk to children as a result of growing up in a family with one or more gay parents. Conscientious and nurturing adults, whether they are men or women, heterosexual or homosexual, can be excellent parents. The rights, benefits, and protections of civil marriage can further strengthen these families* [19].*"*

Surely what is important here, in the context of human-robot marriage, is that it is not the gay or straight nature of the relationship between the parents which is most important for good parenting, but that both parents are *"conscientious and nurturing"*. And just as a gay or lesbian couple can be perfectly good parents for a child, there seems to me to be no valid reason why a sophisticated robot in decades to come cannot be a partner in the provision of good parenting.

Another factor that can affect the stability and happiness of a child brought up by a same-sex couple is whether or not the couple have a relationship free from the stresses and pressures of social adversity due to their sexual orientation. Many research psychologists have concluded that children benefit when their parents are in a legally-recognized form of relationship which is also accepted and supported by society. The Canadian Psychological Association, for example, has stated that *"the stresses encountered by gay and lesbian parents and their children are more likely the result of the way society treats them than because of any deficiencies in fitness to parent"*. [20] ["Marriage of Same-Sex Couples – 2006 Position Statement" Canadian Psychological Association.] On this basis it seems reasonable to argue that human-robot marriage should be made legal for the benefit of the adopted children of such marriages, since by making them legal the human partner (and arguably the robot) will be less likely to feel or appear to be stressed by society's rejection of their robot marriage.

5   Threshold Requirements for Marriage

In their paper *"Robot Marriage and the Law"*, Mark Goldfeder and Yosef Razin discuss three threshold requirements for marriage, requirements that robots will have to meet in order for human-robot marriages to qualify for legalized status [21]. These requirements are: consent, understanding, and the capacity to make decisions.

Consent
An interesting question relating to consent arose in a 2012 case in the Seattle area, in which Angela Marie Vogel became the first woman in American history to marry a corporation. The bride had undertaken this attempt in order to draw attention to the decision, in 2010, by the U.S. Supreme Court, to recognize a corporation as a person. Vogel's marriage did not last long. King's County, where Seattle is located, changed its mind over its earlier decision to allow the marriage to go ahead, and rapidly declared the marriage licence, which it had issued, to be void. A King's County spokesperson explained: *"When either party to a marriage is incapable of consent then it's void, no longer valid, or not valid period"*. So the county's ultimate decision on the matter was that a corporation is not able consent to something. But is that true when extending the rule to a robot? If a robot had been granted personhood then it would seem to be legally eligible to marry, if it chose to do so. And if the robot appeared to wish to marry, by virtue of what it said and how it behaved, then following Turing's philosophy, why should we not assume that it consents?

Goldfeder and Razin [21] identify three fundamental requirements to demonstrate consent:

(a) The parties must have the legal capacity to contract a marriage;
(b) The parties must voluntarily assent to contract a marriage;
(c) There must be at least substantial compliance with statutory requirements as to the formalities of a ceremonial marriage.

The authors argue that a person can indicate their understanding of what marriage means, simply by responding positively to a statement such as "Let's get married". How much understanding is that? Not very much. As the Supreme Court of the state of Arkansas ruled in a 2008 decision, consent does not have to be particularly informed or well-reasoned.

Goldfeder and Razin apply this concept to robots and conclude that *"Sophisticated robots are more than capable of instrumental reasoning, that is, performing cost-benefit analysis and deciding on the best way to proceed in the furtherance of their own best interests."* [21] In the context of robot marriage this means that robots are more than capable of deciding or consenting to marry.

Another important aspect of consent is that it should be genuine, given freely, without coercion. One could argue that if a robot was pre-programmed to consent then such consent would have been obtained through coercion, which in many jurisdictions would render a marriage contract invalid. *"Thus a robot would have to be free to learn and to choose whether it wished to marry, based on internally formed preferences. However, given such freedom, robots could then be unduly influenced by threats or coercion, just like a human"* [21].

Understanding

"Can robots understand the concept of marriage?", ask Goldfeder and Razin. I don't intend this talk to enter a philosophical debate on whether or not robots will be able to understand linguistic meanings. Instead I shall rely, as I often do, on the Turing Test. This leads us to the conclusion that if a robot appears, by its behaviour, both actions and words, to understand the meaning of marriage, then we should accept at face value that the robot does indeed have that level of understanding.

Decisions

The capacity to make decisions is a third requirement for a "robot person" to be allowed to marry. A decision to consent to marriage must, of course, be voluntary and not obtained by coercion, but there is no requirement for the decision to be rational, and as Goldfeder and Razin point out, *"It can be impulsive"* [21]. For more than half a century now, artificial intelligence programs have been able to to perform well at tasks that require planning and decision making, and many such software systems have demonstrated their superiority over the decision-making skills of leading human experts. Given that software can decide which move to make in a chess game better than a human World Champion, it is difficult to deny the possibility that the robots of future decades will be able be able to decide who they "want" to marry.

How robots will evaluate and then decide upon various marriage options is not yet clear, but what will be required of robots making such decisions does not include having a sophisticated value system. It will be sufficient, for the purposes of legality, for the robot to be able to evaluate the pros and cons of entering into an agreement to marry.

Goldfeber and Razin point out that current A.I. systems appear to satisfy reasonable tests for competent decision-making. They further point out that:

> *"Humans are presumed to have mental capacity over a certain age, and, at least from that point on, a right to a competency evaluation. If we adopt similar tests for A.I., it would not be unreasonable to presume a status quo that a given A.I. does not have mental capacity unless meeting the requirements of the test, and competency evaluation may be compulsory. However, once a robot's mental capacity and legal competence are established, it is presumed that they can freely consent, unless coerced or the robot's functionality is compromised [21]."*

A robot person who is legally permitted to, and capable of, entering into a legal contract, *"could certainly understand, decide and express an intention to enter into a marriage contract"*, and appear to be happy as a result. If the robot appears to be happy in its marriage, where's the harm for the robot?

In questioning whether a robot should be *allowed* by law to marry a human, Goldfeder and Razin point out that case law has been moving towards equating the actions of human beings, when considering the mental state of a robot for legal purposes. If a robot's behaviour suggests that it is in a particular mental state, then we should presume that it is so. If a robot's behaviour suggests that it wishes to marry, then we should treat it as though it does so wish.

But it is the complimentary question which forms the title of this talk. *"Why not marry a robot?"* As professor Gary Marchant has opined: *"Robot-human marriage is not about robot rights. It is about the right of a <u>human</u> to choose to marry a robot"* [22].

6 Conclusion

The title of my book, the name of this conference, is now one of the most talked about topics in the field of social robotics. Love, sex and marriage have undergone enormous changes as discussion topics since the mid-20th century, not only changes in society's attitudes to them but also in terms of people's willingness to talk about them openly. Even a single generation ago it would have been almost unthinkable to organize a conference like this one. But with advances coming thick and fast in computing, in A.I. in general, and in robotics in particular, we are being forced to contemplate what human-robot relationships will be like a generation or two from now. As Sherry Turkle asks, in her book *"Alone Together"*, asking about how technology will change us, what will we be like? What type of people will we become? [23] Transposing Turkle's question to social robotics it could be paraphrased as "How will we come to regard robots? What will our relationships with them be like? And just how far will our relationships with them extend?

In my book and elsewhere there can be found ample explanations as to how and why many people will be falling in love with robots during the coming decades. And sex with robots is just around the corner, with the first sexbots coming from Abyss Creations in California some time next year. As love and sex with robots become more and more commonplace, not only as subjects for academic and public discussion but also in practice, so we shall come face to face with the very real possibility of marriage to robots. When robots are sufficiently humanlike and sufficiently appealing socially, to the point where they can act as our companions, why not extend that companionship to marriage, if neither party is against the idea?

Today I have addressed some issues of personhood in the Law - whether robots will come to be regarded as having personhood, as being some type of person, I have presented some examples from the literature, examples of ways in which society's ethical and legal views relating to personhood and the law are changing, and will, inevitably, change even faster with future developments in robot and software technologies.

As more and more people come to accept the concepts of sex and love with robots, so society as a whole will develop laws to govern human-robot relationships. And as those laws evolve, the type of legal restriction which prevented Angela Marie Vogel from obtaining a legally valid marriage licence in Seattle, to allow her to marry a corporation, such laws will begain to fall by the wayside, just as the laws preventing interracial marriage did in 1960 s America, and those relating to same-sex marriage have done during the current decade.

By the time there are no laws to prevent human-robot marriages, robots will be patient, kind, protective, loving, trusting, truthful, persevering, respectful, uncomplaining, complimentary, pleasant to talk to, and sharing your sense of humour. And the robots of the future will not be jealous, boastful, arrogant, rude, self-seeking or easily angered, unless of course you want them to be.

So when the law allows it, why not marry a robot?

Thank you!

References

1. Levy, D.: A history of machines with sexual functions: Past, present and robot. In: EURON Workshop on Roboethics, Genova, Italy, March 2006
2. Levy, D.: Emotional relationships with robotic companions. In: EURON Workshop on Roboethics, Genova, Italy, March 2006
3. Levy, D.: Marriage and sex with robots. In: EURON Workshop on Roboethics, Genova, Italy, March 2006
4. Levy, D.: Love and Sex with Robots. HarperCollins, New York (2007)
5. Levy, D.: Intimate Relationships with Artificial Partners. Ph.D. Thesis, University of Maastricht (2007)
6. Freitas Jr., R.: The legal rights of robots. Student Lawyer **13**, 54–56 (1985)
7. Wettig, S., Zehendner, E.: The electronic agent: A legal personality under German law. In: Proceedings of the Law and Electronic Agents workshop (LEA 2003), p. 97 (2003)
8. Chopra, S., White, L.F.: A Legal Theory for Autonomous Artificial Agents. University of Michigan Press, Ann Arbor (2011)
9. Hubbard, F.P.: Do androids dream?: Personhood and intelligent artifacts. Temple Law Rev. **83**, 405–494 (2010)
10. Sparrow, R.: Can machines be people? Reflections on the turing triage test. In: Lin, P., Abney, K., Bekey, G. (eds.) Robot Ethics: The Ethical and Social Implications of Robotics, pp. 301–315. MIT Press (2012)
11. Muzyka, K.: The outline of personhood law regarding artificial intelligences and emulated human entities. J. Artif. Gen. Intell. **4**(3), 164–169 (2014)
12. Zimmerman, E.: Machine Minds: Frontiers in Legal Consciousness (2015). Available at SSRN: https://ssrn.com/abstract=2563965 or http://dx.doi.org/10.2139/ssrn.2563965

13. Leroux, C., et al.: Suggestions for a green paper on legal issues in robotics. In: EU Robotics, The European Robotics Coordination Action (2012)
14. Stone, L.S.: Gay Marriage and Anthropology. Anthropology News, May 2004
15. Rule, S.: Rights for Gay Couples in Denmark. The New York Times, 2 October 1989
16. Scocca, T.: Newt Gingrich on Gay Marriage: Shameless and/or Fearless (2010). Slate [a blog] Available at http://www.slate.com/blogs/scocca/2010/08/05/newt_gingrich_on_gay_marriage_shameless_and_or_fearless.html
17. Defence of Marriage Act (1996). https://www.gpo.gov/fdsys/pkg/PLAW-104publ199/html/PLAW-104publ199.htm
18. Southern Baptist Convention resolutions (2003). http://www.sbc.net/resolutions/1128
19. Pawelski, J.G., et al.: The effects of marriage, civil union, and domestic partnership laws on the health and well-being of children. Pediatrics **118**(1), 349–364 (2006)
20. Marriage of Same-Sex Couples – 2006 Position Statement. Canadian Psychological Association (2006). http://www.cpa.ca/cpasite/userfiles/Documents/Marriage%20of%20Same-Sex%20Couples%20Position%20Statement%20-%20October%202006%20(1).pdf
21. Goldfeder, M., Razin, Y.: Robotic marriage and the law. J. Law Soc. Deviance **10**(12), 137–176 (2015)
22. Marchant, G.: A.I. Thee Wed (2015). Slate [a blog] Available at http://www.slate.com/articles/technology/future_tense/2015/08/humans_should_be_able_to_marry_robots.html
23. Turkle, S.: Alone Together. Basic Books, Philadelphia (2011)

Papers

Sex Robots from the Perspective of Machine Ethics

Oliver Bendel[✉]

School of Business FHNW, Bahnhofstrasse 6, 5210 Windisch, Switzerland
oliver.bendel@fhnw.ch

Abstract. This contribution explains firstly the terms and the phenomena of sex robots and robot sex and the foundations of machine ethics. Secondly it poses questions related to sex robots as moral agents, from a general and a specific perspective, aiming at assisting manufacturers and developers. By using the questions, the opportunities and risks can be discussed in a structured manner. Thirdly, the fields of applied ethics are included to work out the implications for humans as moral patients. At the end, the author summarizes the findings. Machine ethics, from his point of view, may help to construct sex robots and service robots with special capabilities which are moral machines in their appearance and in their behaviour and which may allow some people to complement their sexual activities and to lead a fulfilling life. The fields of applied ethics may be beneficial with respect to the adequate use of sex robots.

Keywords: Sex robots · Sex dolls · Robot sex · Artificial intelligence · Machine ethics · Technology ethics · Information ethics

1   Introduction

The present contribution explains firstly the terms and the phenomena of sex robots and robot sex and the foundations of machine ethics. Secondly it poses questions related to sex robots as moral agents to assist manufacturers and developers. Those are evaluated and explained in detail. Thirdly, the specific ethics (i.e., the fields of applied ethics) are included to work out the implications for humans as moral patients. At the end, the author summarizes the findings.

The analysis of sex robots and robotic sex has become a tradition [13–15, 24]. Robotics, psychology, criminology and sexology all contribute to it, but machine ethics as a consistent perspective is lacking. Some stand-alone questions have been raised in the literature related to the discipline, and there are a few systematic lists of requirements [4]; but there is no pertinent analysis or classification. This article wants to close this gap.

2   Robotic Sex and Sex Robots

Robotic sex, as sex with and among robots, is a subject of science fiction, both literature and film, and of computer games. Today it is also considered for healthcare, for instance to assist handicapped or elderly people, and to support therapies [4]. Newspapers and magazines are enthusiastic about robotic sex [13, 14], and eager academic discussions

© Springer International Publishing AG 2017
A.D. Cheok et al. (Eds.): LSR 2016, LNAI 10237, pp. 17–26, 2017.
DOI: 10.1007/978-3-319-57738-8_2

are going on about it. Sex with robots, within the meaning of sex between man and machine, is usually handled through sex robots, but other service and even industrial robots also come to question. Sex robots can be defined as robots designed and programmed for the purpose of sex with all kinds of interested and capable people – men and women, gays and lesbians, black and white, teenagers and adults, frail and gross people.

Depending on budget and taste, sex machines and robots are available as a handy toy or as a life-size shape [4]. They help people reach fun and satisfaction through stimulation or penetration. Some have natural language skills and arousing voices, and one should not forget that verbal eroticism is very popular in chats, and phone sex was in high demand for a long time and still is in existence. The sexual interactions in virtual reality applications can also be used for comparison. The advantages of sex robots are their constant availability, the low risk of disease transmission if handled correctly, and unburdening of sex workers of all genders. Their drawbacks are the limited bandwidth of availability and satisfaction, the high risk of disease transmission if handled not correctly, and the current low acceptance by the population.

There are several products and approaches. Just a few examples may suffice. Roxxxy is a sexbot which according to information from the company's website (www.true-companion.com) is able to listen and speak and to respond to touching. Several person-alities can be chosen from, ranging from "Wild Wendy" to "Frigid Farrah". The male equivalent is called Rocky, the name reminiscent of the famous film figure. Companies like Abyss Creations (www.realdoll.com) and Doll Sweet (www.dsdolleurope.com) try to develop lifelike love dolls with convincing skin and flesh [3], and some of them investigate potentials of sex robots. In 2015, media reported that the manufacturer of Pepper cautioned against sex with its conventional service robot [26]. This shows that not only genuine sex robots and love dolls are candidates in this field.

3   The Discipline of Machine Ethics

Machine ethics is a young and dynamic scientific discipline with representatives all over the world. It refers to the morality of semi-autonomous or autonomous machines like service robots, co-robots, chatbots, self-driving cars or certain civil respectively military drones [1, 25]. Hence these machines are new and strange moral agents. They decide and act in situations where they are left alone, either by following pre-defined rules or by comparing the situations to selected case models, or as machines capable of learning [5].

The term of morality in this context has been criticized by scientists and journalists, although it is explicitly referenced to machines, and does not imply that machines behave to the same extent as humans [4]. At least the term "morality" can be applied to machines metaphorically (machine morality is different from human morality, but there are some similarities) or intentionally (one day machine morality will be more or less like human morality).

While the classical special fields of applied ethics rather are reflective disciplines, machine ethics is more of a design discipline, and as such it is close to robotics and artificial intelligence, or to information science respectively. Some machine ethicists prioritize on designing simulations and prototypes in order to prove the possibility of moral machines or the underlying theoretical assumptions [7, 18].

4 The Perspective of Machine Ethics

In the section below, questions referring to sex robots and robotic sex are posed and discussed from the perspective of machine ethics. As empirical studies are virtually non-existent, analysis of literature, argumentation chains or conclusions are methods of choice. More general questions are posed at the beginning, followed by more specific ones. These might help responsible persons in companies or programmers to develop solutions in forms agreeable to society and individual. Managers of institutions (such as hospitals, nursing homes, or brothels) also can benefit from the considerations. The intention is not to list only complaints and limitations; the goal is to enable the creation of robots that as an entity fulfil the requirements, demands, and needs of operators, users and affected persons (meaning role models for robots as well as partners or relatives of owners).

4.1 General Questions in the Field of Machine Ethics

Machine ethics is one of several disciplines the design and programming of sex robots can refer to, next to psychology, social robotics, and robotics in general, as well as artificial intelligence and human-machine interaction [3, 10]. The general questions of machine ethics in this context are [4]:

1. Should the sex robot have moral skills, and if yes, which ones?
2. Should it follow defined rules only (duty ethics), or should it be able to estimate the consequences of its actions (consequential ethics) and weigh pros and cons for decision-making?
3. Do other normative models apply, for instance the ethics of virtue or the contract theory?
4. Should the moral machine be implemented as a self-learning system, and if yes, how should it learn?
5. How autonomous should the sex robot be, and for which reason?

The answer to the question whether or not the sex robot should have moral skills (question 1) has to consider the moral situation the human sex partner of the sex robot frequently can be in. He might worry about general questions of the usage, for instance if it is right for his own present and future life, or if the environment might be opposed to it. On the one hand, the robot as a moral machine could reduce the reservations of friends and family by explaining certain aspects; but on the other hand it might stipulate critically analysis of its handling. General moral skills are a consideration, as sexual interaction is embedded in social interaction where good and evil behaviours can always develop.

Models of normative ethics have been discussed with regards to robots for some time (questions 2 and 3). Especially the classical models, linked to Aristotle or Immanuel Kant, seem to be particularly suitable [6]. Thinking in terms of consequence ethics or duty ethics, this might be due to their level of abstraction. Virtue ethics raises special requirements, on the one hand, virtues as such are describable, and on the other hand, they usually are genuinely human characteristics and targets. Other models created in the 19th and 20th century focus even more on the human as a moral agent and moral reference. The existentialist concept founded by Søren Kierkegaard is known as existential ethics. Ethical considerations concentrate on the human existence. Transferring such concepts to machines without strongly modifying the character of these philosophies is difficult.

The question if the moral machine should be designed as a self-learning system leads into deep, controversial discussion (question 4). Some authors think it is advisable, at present or in general, to limit the considerations to simple moral machines or operational moral [8, 25]. For them it is often enough to follow a comprehensive number of rules; often they are underway in semi-open worlds, for instance in households (as vacuuming robots that spare animals), or in parkways (as mowing robots that spare flora and fauna). In open worlds, for instance in traffic or at war, more complex machines seem to be necessary, and high learning capacity contributes to enable them to rate more and more situations, but there is disagreement on whether this kind of development of the morality of machines is purposive. Is sexual interaction a moral situation that is easy to overview or impossible to overview? This depends on the human sex partner and on his or her ability to change and learn. It is safe to assume that a complex person will require a complex machine, but this does not mean it will be able in the end to satisfy particularly well, or to make the human happy. Maybe adjustability is just as important in sexuality as in moral matters.

The degree of autonomy of sex robots again depends on their application and on the user profile (question 5). In terms of sexuality, one can distinguish passive and active behaviour. An active human might be satisfied with a passive counterpart, while a passive human might want a more active one. Autonomy and morality generally are closely interrelated; the same can be said for machines. An autonomous system comes into many different situations, some of them are morally charged, and it has to be able to rate and master them on its own. Vice versa, complex situations might overwhelm autonomous machines. It is possible to create sex robots that are able to master standard situations and in extreme situations would recommend or obtain human support, either from their counterparts or from uninvolved persons. The prerogative is to classify situations in normative terms in advance, and this is possible on principle. The GOODBOT, a chatbot developed out of machine ethics in a project at the School of Business FHNW in 2013/2014, for instance was taught to recognize problems of the user, if expressed by speech, and to escalate them on three levels [7]. On the highest level, it will give out a national emergency hotline number. This would be an adequate action also for a sex robot to take in case of medical or psychological problems.

4.2 Specific Questions in the Field of Machine Ethics

Some general questions have been posed and discussed. There are also more specific questions, when we focus on the sex partner in a stronger way and when we consider not only the robot's behaviour but also its appearance [4]:

6. Should the robot become active on its own, and entice the partner to have sex?
7. Should it be able, in extreme cases, to refuse performing the act?
8. Should it make clear to the human being that it is no more than a machine?
9. Should design and realization fulfil moral criteria, for instance should child-like sex robots be prohibited?
10. Should the appearance be "politically correct", in terms of race and ethnicity, and what does this mean concretely?
11. Should there be novelty options for stimulation and seduction, or should the sex robots follow human role models?
12. Should conventional service robots feature extensions to enhance the possibilities or should they be as "unsexual" and "neutral" as possible?

Whether or not the robot should become active on its own, and entice its partner to have sex (question 6), relates to the already discussed issue of autonomy and activity or passivity. Here, the more specific question is in how far the sex robot should be an initiator, a seducer, or a driver. This leads to questions about the relation between human sexuality and machine sexuality. Human sexuality has physical limits, and especially male sexuality is limited by increasing age. If the sex robot overexerts its counterpart, the counterpart will hardly have opportunity to have intercourse with human partners. Other physical and psychic aspects are caused by exhaustion and strain. Falling into normative categories is too simple. Once one has decided to sexually interact and communicate with preference with machines, there is no reason why moral aspects should be over-emphasized. The only aspect worthy of discussion would be in how far a partner, who was given a promise on the type of relationship, either implicitly or explicitly, would be neglected or repelled by the interaction. Of course, one may submit recommendations for the implementation in order to prevent extreme loads. Machine ethics could help to realize sex robots which do not overexert their counterparts.

The question of rejection and refusal by the machine (question 7) is interesting not only in the sexual context, but also in contexts where criminal deeds or morally inadequate actions are at disposal. Again, this is related to the matter of autonomy. The extent of autonomy would be high enough for the machine to cast off its tool-like character and to be an actor on its own, if without free will or self-confidence. An act of refusal could let the machine appear more human, with all the advantages and disadvantages this entices, and demonstrate that limits in interactions with machines must not necessarily dissolve, but could be defined by responsible persons to be implemented by machines. On the one hand, this could be interpreted as an indication of the sexual autonomy of humans the user still might have interaction with; on the other hand, it could lead to frustration, especially if the user has suffered rejection from humans repeatedly before. It is important to reflect these problems before a concretion in machine ethics.

Some experts have requested that machines have to make clear they are only machines (question 8). The "principles of robotics" by Margaret Boden, Joanna Bryson, Darwin Caldwell and others claim with a view to robots that "their machine nature should be transparent" [9]. Oliver Bendel proposes a V-effect for robots, an alienation effect in the tradition of Bertolt Brecht: The human shall be torn out of the illusion every now and then [12]. Illusioning is a very old cultural technique, applied in literature, movies and theatre, and not objectionable as such. However it can be desirable for the user to remain able to judge and criticize political and social conditions, as was the intention of the socialist poet and playwright, or one's own constitution, as is relevant in this context. The sex robot can dampen expectations for feelings and relations, and can show other means for sexual fulfilment beside it. Repeated demonstration of the machine that it is only a machine might lead to perceiving it more than ever as a human being because it has strategies of redundancy and transparency one would not necessarily expect from an artefact, and application of language technologies almost inevitably leads to anthropomorphization. This issue should be further explored in machine ethics and robot ethics.

Machine ethics normally analyses the morality applied in decisions and actions of machines. It can also deal with their visual design, the specification of their outward appearance, and set them in relation to morality (question 9). The question of whether or not sex robots resembling children are permissible is discussed intensively [11]. Taking a look at virtual worlds first is worthwhile. According to reports in the media and from eyewitnesses, adults frequently sexually assault children in Second Life; but it is probably safe to assume the virtual children are played by adults in reality [17]. Obviously these are pertinent role plays or plays with age ("age play"), known from chats and computer games and other spaces. According to the Second Life Wiki (wiki.secondlife.com) child avatars generally are permissible but with several exceptions. "Child avatars in sexual situations (sexual congress obviously, though it is unclear beyond this) are not allowed and abuse reportable…" Also "child avatar nudity of the genital or chest regions, including in otherwise non-sexual situations (skin vendors, for example) can be a violation".

Hardware robots obviously add a physical dimension. Certain behaviour is practiced on a machine of childlike size and features. Users are active virtually by manipulating avatars or figures. In reality, users also use their hands, arms or genitals to manipulate the machine. This can be considered ethically questionable; or medicine, psychology and sexology can be consulted. If childlike sex robots could help reduce sexual abuse of children, they might be an instrument in and beyond therapy. If they increase sexual abuse of children by assisting the training of behaviour in a fictional-real test situation, and this behaviour later unfolds in social reality, they have to be questioned with regard to morality, and legal consequences have to be addressed.

When it comes to visual design, gender, ethnicity (colour of skin and hair), size, weight etc. have to be considered (question 10). If the robot has to have a gender, and a certain gender at that, will the mass of developments have the face or body of a woman? Feminists have objected frequently; they argued that sex robots with female design are technical reductions sacrificing female persons to the male phantasy, making them sexual objects [19, 22]. Today however the sex toy market, which has grown strongly [16],

addresses mainly women, and the conditions have been reversed. Not only are men elim-
inated as sexual partners by vibrators and dildos, they even are reduced to their genitals,
but this has few caused complaints or public discussions. Obviously, it is considered
normal to use an artificial member for stimulation while some social circles are alienated
by the concept of using an artificial human resembling a woman for sexual satisfaction.
Maybe the non-reduction in the technical segment, the full-body representation, is linked
to the reduction in the biological segment, and fully artificial vaginas might be less repul-
sive. Such items are also available on the market, for instance the Deluxe Masturbator
Pussy to Go or the Fleshlight Girl Riley Reid Lotus Male Masturbator, and just as sex
robots, they are debatable, considering that versions like Deluxe Pussy Little Miss are
available which – because of their size or tightness – again lead to the discussion about
age. There are very few findings about the ethnicity of sex robots; it has to be assumed
that the exclusive use of one skin complexion or the total lack of human skin complexion
would cause irritations.

Should there be novelty options for stimulation and seduction or should machines
follow human standards or role models (question 11)? Partly this question again relates
to the visual design, but partly also to the behaviour of machines. Futuristic machines
that arouse and satisfy new sexual needs are a topic of science fiction books and movies;
and machines such as Fuckzilla contribute to a better understanding of the exact options
[4]. David Levy and Georg Seeßlen have shown that pertinent artefacts have differed
from human standards for centuries [15, 23]. If a machine is furnished with more than
two hands and two breasts and several genitals etc. users might get used to this plurality,
and be disappointed when this is not found on a real person. The user might also be
repulsed, or amused, by the additional options. Of course such speculations have to be
overcome by interviews and tests. In total, a variety of appearance and behaviour might
be fruitful, and inspire human relationships, even if they don't apply technology.

It was shown in different real-world contexts that robots can be applied to other than
the designed purposes [2]. The police for instance has used service robots in order to
eliminate criminals [21]. The user manual of a humanoid robot called Pepper says, as
already mentioned, that users must not subject it to sexual activities [26]. Otherwise
penalties would apply, but which penalties would apply, or who would execute them is
not specified, and how the manufacturer plans to uncover sexual activities performed
on the robot it is not at all explained. This already indicates the relevance of questions
from special fields of applied ethics, for instance on the monitoring or informational
autonomy. The limbs and body parts one could have sex with remain unclear. SoftBank
Mobile Corp. took its warning even further, and beyond the body. Software adjustments
for giving Pepper an erotic voice are forbidden. It is interesting that the French-Japanese
product shows emotions, and stimulates emotions in others. It seems these emotions
shall be restricted to a tight corset and not destined for falling in love and getting tangled
up and trapped.

The question is should the design of service robots be generalistic so they could be
used for sexual interaction and communication, or should they even have special tools
to predestine them for this purpose (question 12). This leads to the next question: are
special sex robots necessary, or could certain service robots be used for the purpose,
considering how this would lower the inhibitions to purchase and operate one.

Companies like Abyss Creations and Doll Sweet show the outer appearance can be taken very far to create strong sexual connotations through visual design alone. In order to realize such an effect, but not to overemphasize it, service robots would have to be furnished with digital elements such as displays. This is done to simplify facial expression, but under certain circumstances this might limit haptic options as well as physical stimulations.

5   The Perspective of the Fields of Applied Ethics

Machine ethics as a design discipline seems to be crucial in developing adequate sex robots, but applied ethics with its reflection approaches is also important. Below some questions from this perspective [4]:

13. How to process the data the sex robot collects and evaluates to better satisfy the partner's needs or to inform companies?
14. Who is liable for injuries or contamination caused by the use of the machines?
15. How to handle frustration, uncertainty, shame, disgrace and jealousy caused by the sex robot?
16. It is possible to be unfaithful to the human love partner with a sex robot, and can a man or a woman be jealous because of the robot's other love affairs?
17. Does the robot replace, complement or support a human partner?
18. Is robotic sex an indication of raw and crude tendencies, e.g., by promoting the idea that a sex partner has to be available at all times?
19. Should sex robots be available everywhere, and should it be possible to use them everywhere and anytime?
20. Should children and teenagers be permitted to have access to sex robots, and, if so, under which circumstances?

These questions might be answered from the perspective of information, technology, business, medical and sexual ethics. Partly they are also related to legal matters. Responsible persons in companies (CEOs and managers), programmers, and legislators could benefit therefrom.

Intensive discussion cannot take place in this article because of the limited length. The first question shall be discussed briefly because it was touched in the last paragraph (question 13), as well as the last one, especially because it seems so unusual and unambiguous. Some robots, like security robots, have been developed purposively for surveillance and monitoring. The K5 and the K3 from Knightscope recognize abnormalities, and report them to a headquarter [20]. What if the sex robot or a robot used for sex is just as indiscreet? What if it collects and discloses information on sexual practices, or records them in audio or visual form, and disseminates the recordings? There might be rational and functional reasons for data collection and recording, for instance for product improvement or the detection of weaknesses or errors. On the one hand, endangering the autonomy of information is potentially detrimental to the user; on the other hand, it is detrimental to the acceptance of sex robots. A childlike sex robot might report being used outside of therapy, and warn of imminent danger. An adult one might report being beaten and hurt, which could be interpreted as crossing a border and worthy of more detailed investigation. Sending out artificial spies to explore human sex life however would be a kind of abuse in itself.

As already mentioned this article does not go into questions 14, 15, 16, 17, 18 and 19. Should children and teenagers be granted access to sex robots (question 20)? Obviously the answer to this question is simply no. There are many reasons why children should make their very first sexual experiences, if at all, with other children. Doctor games with robots would be played in a certain imbalance. Children cannot really discover the other gender, or their own gender in relation to another person, they can only detect metal, silicone, and programming versions. Not to forget question 13 as discussed in the previous paragraph. Guiding kids towards technologies that might spy them out is dangerous, and it is also unfair if they cannot see through, or overview and estimate, the products and processes. The same can be said for teens, especially relating to the very first sexual experience. But what if they already had been sexually active, but cannot be sufficiently active for what reason so ever? Perhaps there are no good reasons not to grand 16 year olds access to sex robots. But we must be very careful regarding the development of adolescents, and in individual cases it might be better to avoid a "first contact" at an early stage.

6 Summary and Outlook

All in all robot sex is a highly sensitive field [4]. Those who are substituted by a focused machine might feel rejected. Those who have to have intercourse with a sex robot for having no other choice might suffer, as well as those who cannot afford such a high-end gadget. The matter raises marginal practical questions, which cannot be analysed in depth here. A dildo or vibrator can be stored discreetly, a sex robot cannot. Only very few relationships will be able to integrate a machine like that.

Machine ethics may help to construct sex robots which are moral machines in their appearance and in their behaviour. After the right questions have been posed, the right answers have to be provided, which is the job of machine ethicists, roboticists and sex experts – and of the whole society. This article raised and discussed questions from the perspective of machine ethics, and partly from selected special fields of applied ethics. Here and there it was possible to give answers and propose solutions.

References

1. Anderson, M., Anderson, S.L. (eds.): Machine Ethics. Cambridge University Press, Cambridge (2011)
2. Bendel, O.: Überlegungen zur Zweckentfremdung von Robotern. In: inside-it.ch, 18 August 2016. http://www.inside-it.ch
3. Bendel, O.: Die Sexroboter kommen: Die Frage ist nur, wie und wann. In: Telepolis, 13 June 2016. http://www.heise.de/tp/artikel/48/48471/1.html
4. Bendel, O.: Surgical, therapeutic, nursing and sex robots in machine and information ethics. In: van Rysewyk, S.P., Pontier, M. (eds.) Machine Medical Ethics, pp. 17–32. Springer, New York (2015)

5. Bendel, O.: Wirtschaftliche und technische Implikationen der Maschinenethik. Die Betriebswirtschaft **4**, 237–248 (2014)
6. Bendel, O.: Towards machine ethics. In: Michalek, T., Hebáková, L., Hennen, L., et al. (eds.) Technology Assessment and Policy Areas of Great Transitions. 1st PACITA Project Conference, 13–15 March 2013, Prague, pp. 321–326 (2014)
7. Bendel, O.: Good bot, bad bot: Dialog zwischen Mensch und Maschine. UnternehmerZeitung **7**(19), 30–31 (2013)
8. Bendel, O.: Ich bremse auch für Tiere: Überlegungen zu einfachen moralischen Maschinen. In: inside-it.ch, 4 December 2013. http://www.inside-it.ch/articles/34646
9. Boden, M., Bryson, J., Caldwell, D.: Principles of robotics: Regulating robots in the real world. Guidelines for engineers and roboticists from a EPSRC/AHRC funded retreat (2010). https://www.epsrc.ac.uk/research/ourportfolio/themes/engineering/activities/principlesofrobotics/
10. Coeckelbergh, M.: Personal robots, appearance, and human good: a methodological reflection on roboethics. Int. J. Soc. Robot. **1**(3), 217–221 (2009)
11. Danaher, J.: Robotic rape and robotic child sexual abuse: should they be criminalised? In: Criminal Law and Philosophy, pp. 1–25, 13 December 2014
12. Freuler, R.: Was hat Sex mit Technologie zu tun? In: NZZ am Sonntag, pp. 60–61, 23 October 2016
13. Hänßler, B.: Stets zu Liebesdiensten. In: Stuttgarter-Zeitung.de, 29 August 2012. http://www.stuttgarter-zeitung.de/inhalt.sexroboter-stets-zu-liebesdiensten.59ec16f3-55c3-4bef-a7ba-d24eccfa8d47.html
14. Hartwell, L.: So who wants to f**k a robot? In: Wired.com, 10 June 2007. http://www.wired.com/underwire/2007/10/so-who-wants-to/
15. Levy, D.: Sex and Love with Robots. The Evolution of Human-Robot Relationships. Harper Perennial, New York (2008)
16. Möthe, A.: Sexspielzeug statt Tupperware. In: Handelsblatt, 27 February 2015. http://www.handelsblatt.com/unternehmen/handel-konsumgueter/boom-der-erotik-branche-sexspielzeug-statt-tupperware/11430194.html
17. O'Hear, S.: Second Life child pornography investigation. In: ZDNet, 10 May 2007. http://www.zdnet.com/article/second-life-child-pornography-investigation/
18. Pereira, L.M., Saptawijaya, A.: Programming Machine Ethics. Springer, Cham (2016)
19. Richardson, K.: The asymmetrical 'Relationship': parallels between prostitution and the development of sex robots. SIGCAS Comput. Soc. **45**(3), 290–293 (2015)
20. Rötzer, F.: Chinas erster Überwachungsroboter. In: Telepolis, 13 May 2016. http://www.heise.de/tp/artikel/48/48232/1.html
21. Rötzer, F.: Dallas: Umfunktionierter Bombenroboter zur gezielten Tötung eines Verdächtigen. In: Telepolis, 8 July 2016. http://www.heise.de/tp/artikel/48/48771/1.html
22. Scheutz, M., Arnold, T.: Are we ready for sex robots? In: HRI 2016: The Eleventh ACM/IEEE International Conference on Human Robot Interaction, March 2016, pp. 351–358 (2016)
23. Seeßlen, G.: Träumen Androiden von elektronischen Orgasmen? Sex-Fantasien in der Hightech-Welt I. Bertz-Fischer, Berlin (2012)
24. Sullins, J.P.: Robots, love, and sex: the ethics of building a love machine. IEEE Trans. Affect. Comput. **3**(4), 398–409 (2012)
25. Wallach, W., Allen, C.: Moral Machines. Teaching Robots Right from Wrong. Oxford University Press, Oxford (2009)
26. Wendel, J.: Pepper The Robot soll nicht für Sex benutzt werden. In: Wired, 24 September 2015. https://www.wired.de/collection/latest/eine-passage-im-nutzervertrag-von-pepper-robot-verbietet-sex

Affective Labor and Technologies of Gender in Wei Yahua's "Conjugal Happiness in the Arms of Morpheus"

Virginia L. Conn[✉]

Rutgers University, New Brunswick, NJ, USA
Virginia.L.Conn@rutgers.edu

Abstract. Robotics explores the boundary between the human body and its objective use value, recasting the fields of of gender and affect as commodities—a question that takes on specific cultural values in post-Mao China. This privileging of technology and its engagement with gendered labor are examined in Wei Yahua's short story, "Conjugal Happiness in the Arms of Morpheus," which uses the feminine performativity of a robot wife to engage with the intertwined role of affective labor and the legal status of objects. Such a performance decenters the human subject while simultaneously subjugating the laboring technological materials, such that Lili—the robot wife in question—is only capable of acquiring legal subjecthood through her appeal to a law that binds human actors.

The historical context in which this story was written is as important an artifact as the language it uses and the subject matter it treats, raising the specter of a possible ethics of consciousness unconnected to humanistic social mores at a time when technology was being touted as the way towards a collective future emancipated from labor as a whole. In 1980s China, labor and technology were both equally privileged as sites of socialist revolution, with a restructuring of the imaginaries of both free and controlled labor. By raising the question of differential relationships in a supposedly egalitarian society through characters that explore their various relationships to artificial life, "Conjugal Happiness in the Arms of Morpheus" offers a critical look into what kinds of labor (and laboring bodies) are replaceable and which are privileged—and, in doing so, directly critiques the legal framework regarding women in the country, as well as how a subject is defined in the first place.

Keywords: Affective labor · Gender theory and performance · Roboethics · Chinese science fiction · Artificial intelligence

1   Introduction

The mechanized body as a surrogate for human labor—whether emotional or physical—serves as a way to technofantasize old desires of humanization. Informed by legacies of commodification that define the boundaries of the human as gendered and/or laboring, robotics pairs the hope of advancement with the problem of human obsolescence. This is nowhere more true than in texts that explicitly pair technologies of gender with technologies of labor by packaging both in an explicitly feminized mechanical body. Commodification and questions of agency and consciousness are

© Springer International Publishing AG 2017
A.D. Cheok et al. (Eds.): LSR 2016, LNAI 10237, pp. 27–39, 2017.
DOI: 10.1007/978-3-319-57738-8_3

at stake, and, when locating the question within the socialist context of the post-Mao 80s in mainland China, technoscientific embodiment as a framework for social criticism rises to the forefront. This paper will ask questions about what technologies of labor and gender are at work in Wei Yahua's (魏雅华) "Conjugal Happiness in the Arms of Morpheus" and how those two tracks intersect to engineer new possibilities and problems for social (and socialist) realities.

Wei Yahua's 《我决定与机器人妻子离婚》 ("I Decided to Divorce my Robot Wife") and its sequel, 《温柔之乡的梦》 ("Dream of a Soft Country"), collectively translated by Wu Dingbo as "Conjugal Happiness in the Arms of Morpheus," features a male scientist narrator who, in selecting a robot wife, comes to realize that perfect obedience borne out of strict gender roles leads only to misery. Lili—the titular robot wife—is selected from thousands of other models for her "traditional characteristics" of subservience and beauty, as well as obedience in all things. This slavish deference leads her to burning her husband's important papers at his behest, after which he decides to divorce her. In the courtroom scene that ends "I Decided to Divorce my Robot Wife," Lili claims she was just acting as she'd been programmed to, and the divorce does not go forward.

In the follow-up, "Dream of a Soft Country," the narrating husband is approached by a chemist who informs him that, by changing Lili's chemical composition, she will become more humanlike. After being exposed to both a change in her chemical composition and to Western philosophy—Heidegger, Rousseau, Montesquieu, Hegel, Feuerbach, Aristotle, Mendolssohn, and Moleschott are mentioned specifically—Lili accuses her husband of boorishness and demands a divorce on the grounds that she has been nothing for him but a sexual surrogate and slave and that, as a woman, she deserves equal treatment under the law. Her argument is heard in court, and with the support of everyone except the company owner who built her and who claims that granting her emancipation will be devastating for his business, she's granted her divorce.

The true subversiveness of the story, however, does not come from any ideological critique of Chinese social traditions—the story, in fact, was written a mere year after the 1980 Marriage Law was passed, which banned arranged or forced marriages and tried to make the institution of marriage itself more equal by focusing on the interests of women and children, as opposed to reasserting the dominance of husbands. The law, in addition, provided for the right to lawful divorce based on emotional or affective grounds (as opposed to the fault-based moralistic right to divorce granted by the earlier 1950 Marriage Law).[1] Rather, its subversion rises from the feminine performativity of Lili, the robot wife.

2   The Historical Rise and Subsequent Displacement of the Laboring Subject

Before engaging with the techniques employed by Lili to gain her freedom, however, it must be recognized that the historical context in which this story was written is as

---

[1] Tamney, J.B., & Chiang, L.H. (2002). *Modernization, Globalization, and Confucianism in Chinese Societies*. Westport, CT: Praeger.

important an artifact as the language it uses and the subject matter it treats, raising the specter of a possible ethics of consciousness unconnected to humanistic social mores at a time when technology was being touted as the way towards a collective future emancipated from labor. In 1980s China, labor and technology were both equally privileged as sites of socialist revolution, with a restructuring of the imaginaries of both free and controlled labor. By raising the question of differential relationships in a supposedly egalitarian society through characters that explore their differentiated relationships to artificial life, "Conjugal Happiness in the Arms of Morpheus" offers a critical look into what kinds of labor (and laboring bodies) are replaceable and which are privileged—and, in doing so, directly critiques the legal framework regarding women in the country.

This paper is not explicitly concerned with the question of genre and trying to define what is and is not science fiction and what is and is not, historically, a robot in Chinese literature. Yet the fact that an engagement with labor relations, networked agency, and legal discourse over the bodies of women is couched in science fiction is significant. "In China, science fiction writing is institutionally affiliated with the popularization of science, with the result that science fiction activities have all be attached to the China Popular Science Creating Writing Association instead of the Chinese Writers' Association" (Wei 1989, p. xxii). The popularization of science and science fiction is a historically-bounded issue that is part and parcel with the question of labor.

There's a great deal of discussion (primarily among Western scholars) as to when science fiction as a genre officially "began" in China, with significant contributions from nationalistic Chinese scholars tracing its pedigree back to some of the earliest myths and legends of written Chinese history—山海经 (The Book of Mountains and Seas, 500 BCE) or 淮南子 ([Writings of the] Masters of Huainan, 197 BCE), for example, among others. Some argue that the first known story about robotics was written in China in the fourth century—Zhang Zhan's "Tangwen," (307 BCE) which includes a story of a robot able to fool the king with his emotive performance—and again in Zhang Zhuo's seventh-century 朝野佥载 (translated alternately as "The Complete Records of the Court and the Commoners" or "Draft Notes from the Court and the Country"), which includes two stories about automatons.[2] Each of these stories features robots that are so convincingly lifelike that they're able to fool onlookers, who are nevertheless unsatisfied with them once they realize they're not "real." Yet the focus on material and technoscientific progress presages the widespread popularization of science and national technological progress that took place in the wake of the Cultural Revolution, especially following Zhou Enlai's 1961 speech, which called for moderate liberties to be granted to literary and artistic production.

More than a decade later, Deng Xiaoping gave a talk at the 1978 National Scientific Conference about the importance of science and technology on the part of the working class, which brought the idea of scientific advancement as being widely available to the people into public discourse. While Chinese revolutionary novels and films hinted at the future as occurring outside of the representational frame, the scientific literature that arose in the post-Mao thaw explicitly engaged with the material realities of technological

---

[2] According to Wu Dingbo, the stories concern a robotic monk begging alms from passerbys, and another about a robotic girl who entertains a drunkard.

progress, with an emphasis on the enjoyment and leisure that such technological leaps would bring the working class. The worlds of abundance and luxury in scientific literature from the post-revolutionary era depended on the shift from human laboring bodies to the rise of machines that would free the Chinese people from the hardships of their past.

This allowance for human leisure came at the cost of a decentering of the laboring human subject along with a simultaneous subjugation of laboring technological materials. As "[…] an unresolved tension between the exaltation of manual labor and the anticipatory imagination of a laborless world within socialist science-related genres […] Post-Mao science fiction associates manual labor with primitive stages of evolution, defective female robots, and uncouth ways of life. The laboring body is no longer the essential element that defines humanity but rather an obstacle to future developments— the subhuman residue of a technological regime about to be overcome" (Iovene 2014, p. 20). What's most important to the story here, then, is that the science-fiction element —the robot wife created to avert overpopulation and serve a man's emotional and physical needs—self-consciously removes herself from the sphere of the technological and presents herself as a female-gendered individual, with all the associated sexual, social, and legalistic rituals implied.

Lili's self-presentation in "Conjugal Happiness in the Arms of Morpheus" collapses the boundaries between the spheres of the personal/domestic and the public sphere of work and productivity, specifically within its historical context, such that laboring bodies within a historically-situated spatiotemporal reality intersect with technology in surprising ways. While the automaton has been a recurring figure in Chinese literature since the fourth century BCE, its appearance as a feminine wife—the perfect wife, in fact—in 1980s post-Mao literature brings with it questions of social critique and ethics of progress that are inextricable from their socialist environment. The body of Lili is a laboring one, a commodity that is bought and sold at the price of future demographic peace, and her argument for freedom is based on aligning herself with an oppressed (ostensibly) biological community. The laboring body in "Conjugal Happiness in the Arms of Morpheus" is specifically one performing emotional labor; the gendered labor of reproduction is left to biological males and females. What is commodified and purchased in the transaction of a robot wife is not the means of production, but rather an emotional and sexual surrogate that, to be successful, must perform non-quantifiable acts of emotional labor in support of her husband.

As pointed out by Radhika Gajjala and Annapurna Mamidipudi in "Gendering Processes within Technological Environments: A Cyberfeminist Issue," gendering processes occur within communities of technological production that make visible the inapplicability of a Western paradigm of development as imposed upon non-Western contexts. Encounters with material technologies of the West, when encountered in a wholly different socio-economic and cultural context, do not necessarily reinscribe the same meanings as would be engaged with by Western bodies. Rather, the political climate of 1980s China conveys a very different process of technological gendering for robotic bodies in their assertion of sexual performativity than would a robotic female in the 1980s US. Nowhere is this more apparent than in the decoupling of reproductive labor in a Chinese society just beginning to feel the effects of overpopulation from the emotional labor still prized as the bedrock of social stability.

3   What Kinds of Labor are Being Valued, and Who's Performing It?

Lili is an object that is created in order to free her husband from his reproductive responsibilities while still allowing him to satisfy his sexual and emotional urges. Highly eroticized—though deprived of control over her own sexual organs—she does not possess the reproductive capacity of a biologically human female. Her inability to reproduce is touted as a selling point by the factory owner, who insists that her use value lies in her ability to erotically please, not to perpetuate human reproduction (in fact, her sterility is touted to the point of having "saved mankind"). Setting aside the distinction between "real" women as ones who can reproduce and "false" women as ones who cannot, Lili is eroticized by the act of objectification of the female form while excluding its physical flaws. Notably, though the narrator later recants his position on the desirability of a perfectly obedient woman, he never comes to desire or dream of an imperfect female body.

The labor made possible by her body is two-fold, but both appeal to the utopian Chinese dream of a future free from physical labor that simultaneously and concurrently requires the mobilization of labor *en masse* to effect revolutionary change. The dominant ideology of the 80s was one that called for a recognition of past physical labor but placed contemporary citizens in a hierarchical relationship to earlier laboring bodies, which were seen as a necessary part of history that was all the better for having been left behind. In this vein, characters in Wei Yahua's story position themselves hierarchically to robot wives (there are no robot husbands in this text), who allow for a revolutionary freedom from labor on the part of humans but in the process of making it so become, themselves, degraded. The similarities with traditionally-discounted labor considered within the domestic or female sphere are clear: labor considered to be creative, intelligent, or mentally dexterous is reified in the husband—a brilliant scientist doing work for the technological advancement of the country—while emotional and domestic labor—as Lili provides—is commodified and degraded. More than that, it replicates an ideological reproductive system gendered so that some labor is just reproducing life and culture that's already been created somewhere else, while other, "higher" forms of labor are prized for creative and adaptive intelligence.

The concept of the automaton, then, culminates in a reflection of the destructive potential of a confrontation between humanity and machinery. Attempts to resolve this disconnect necessarily involve the exploration of the effects and affects of the modern era in terms of personal identity, interpersonal/inter-computer communication, power dynamics in terms of globalized new media/technology access, and the fundamental link between technology and a humanity that is growing increasingly dependent on it. For the better part of the story, Lili serves as an artifact that reinscribes the female body as one that labors in deference to male creative genius, and whose labor is barely even noticed as such. In her perfect obedience to her husband and master, she allows for the continued functioning of the world machine that relies on commodified labor to advance the elite while promoting a myth of universal progress.

Expressions of hope for a utopian and egalitarian society produce a degraded and non-human object that reproduces gendered and racialized tropes even while it claims to be liberating; it allows the man narrating the story to miss the turning of the gears that no longer require the operator. As Jurgen Habermas said about the failure of the techno-utopian dream of liberation, "Capitalism is the first mode of production in world history to institutionalize self-sustaining economic growth. It has generated an industrial system that could be freed from the institutional framework of capitalism and connected to mechanisms other than that of the utilization of capital in private form" (Habermas 2005, p. 67). As an artificial intelligence that potentially surpasses humanity while claiming subjectivity through an appeal to the market and the law, Lili becomes the ultimate monkeywrench.

What is fundamentally at stake in both the AI question in general and "Conjugal Happiness in the Arms of Morpheus" in particular is the issue of consciousness versus commodification, and the definitions of consciousness that are "deserving" of rights. Wei Yahua's texts implicitly ask the question of whether all consciousnesses, even if recognized as such, are subsequently and necessarily recognized as equal. A historically patriarchal society's conception of consciousness is, as feminist theorists such as Hélène Cixous[3] have pointed out, one of binary opposition, in which consciousness is defined in opposition to the other—the Other, being, of course, woman. So much more so for artificial intelligence, which *a priori* exists outside the biological gender binary, though it serves much the same role as Woman—to raise a consciousness of self in Man that cannot exist without recognition of the unconsciousness of the Other. To award recognition of consciousness to something that has been created to serve Man—whether that be woman or machine—is to inherently unsettle and displace the locus of consciousness.

Questions such as whether a human being is a kind of machine and whether or not "the mechanical represent[s] the way to our empowerment and perfectibility or to debasement and the loss of what is vital and unique about being human" (Kang 2011, p. 13) indicate the fundamental failure to disrupt the humanistic concept of agency by positing a loss of unique vitality possessed only by humans. For artificial intelligences to convince humans that their responses are also human, they must tie them biologically to human responses, resulting in a scenario in which technological consciousnesses posing a threat to humans through their very existence are a priori defined as unethical. An AI exhibiting autonomy that isn't serving human needs is cast as fundamentally problematic or incomplete at best and, at worst, actively dangerous. To recognize a consciousness that does not recognize humanity as ontologically central to existence is

---

[3] Cixous, in "La Jeune Née," identifies thought itself as structured through oppositions and binaries that are fundamentally hierarchized; not only do these hierarchies orient us towards a gendered system of knowledge, but, further, these binaries are *inherently* hierarchized—that is, they exist only in relation to one another, with one always and automatically taking precedent over the other. The relationship between the coupled concepts are themselves based on a movement that destroys the couple, and the victory, of course, is to come out on top (as it were) in the historical division between man and women, in which woman, ultimately, has no place.

frightening, radical, and revolutionary, as technological development leading to AI in the first place promises that the next teleological step is overcoming the human itself.

As with much of Chinese science fiction, both during the '80s and before, Wei Yahua looked to the West for a certain degree of inspiration, drawing on Isaac Asimov's Three Laws of Robotics as a central conceit. This is laid out explicitly in the opening scene in which the narrator goes to the Universal Robot Company to pick out a wife and sees the laws inscribed on a plaque at the center of the store.

The manager goes on to explain that humans answer instructions according to the logical procedure of "instruction—analysis—decision (resist or execute)—action," (Wei 1989, p. 12) while a robot's logical process is simpler: "instruction—execution" (Wei 1989, p. 12). This simplified procedure is exactly what leads to disaster, when Lili's unquestioning obedience and inability to resist her husband's orders leads her to burn his research at his drunken command. While the precepts of Asimov's Three Laws of Robotics are central to the being and creation of the robot wives in this story, such simplified obedience and slavish inequality between human and non-human actors is later decried as fundamentally flawed—"Although his [Asimov's] Three Laws of Robotics have a reasonable kernel, they also have the seeds of their own damnation" (Wei 1989, p. 26). Not only is this a judgement passed on Lili, specifically, but also indicates the movement of Chinese science fiction away from its own earlier dependence on Western literary and technological precedence.

This issue is particularly important in the context of China, which had nationally mobilized a vast labor force to essentially build the country from scratch only to subsequently offer the promise of freedom from labor through technology. Technology, painted with a broad brush, was held out with the promise of freeing the people from unimaginative, repetitive labor that made both the laborer and his/her labor invisible and extended the history of an autonomous subject whose freedom is in fact only possible through the invisible gendered labor of servants, wives, slaves, etc., with robots in particular being an anthropomorphic object of interest in the early 1980s Chinese popular media. "Although news on the latest models on the market was widely reported and Asimov's stories were debated, writers and critics of science fiction repeatedly emphasized their lack of human intelligence: robots can only do what they are programmed to do" (Iovene 2014, p. 38). Such labor celebrated the strong distinction between the mind as disembodied intellect and allowing for the formation of a new intellectual class.

Such a worldview conflates two materialist issues: a wish for freedom from labor, but also a reproduction of the laboring world in which technology is conceived of and developed only to do what humans already do. In such a situation, recognizing the consciousness of non-human actors stood as a potential obstacle to social progress even if it would potentially result in economic or political progress. The shift in emphasis from individual agency to collective agency had just begun to recognize women as equal members of society—no wonder, then, that Lili finds recognition of her rights in womanhood but not in her status as a robot.

4   Performing the Labor of Being a Woman

In choosing to base her claim for equal rights on her performativity of "woman" as such, Lili relies on Teresa de Laurentis' assertion that gender is a representation. To pose the question of gender in terms of sexual difference is to remain bound by traditional patriarchal notions of othering, which—as with the recognition of artificial intelligence—centers man and posits women as that which is not man. The conflation of gender and sexual difference relies on cultural discourses drawing from medicine, the law, philosophy, and literature, and is grounded in our daily performative rituals and repetitions. Following her exposure to great works within all these categories, Lili becomes excruciatingly aware of the technologies of sexuality and the structures of oppression that have made wives into objects and objects into wives.

Parveen Adams states that "the feminine subject relies on a homogeneous oppression of women in a state, reality, given prior to representational practices" (Adams and Cowie 1990, p. 56). The necessity of a uniformly-oppressed class that is recognized as such under the law is central to Lili's claim to subjectivity, as she draws on the concept of belonging to an oppressed class of women as the basis for her argument towards liberation, rather than insisting on the a-genderedness of herself as a robot. The argument, as she presents it to the court, is not about commodification and her status as a thing, but rather, rests on the fact that women as a class have been repressed and that she belongs to that class, so freedom from the tyranny of oppressive marriage, which was being granted to women, was also hers by dint of belonging to said class.

This argument relies on both Lili's presentation and self-representation as a woman as well as on juridical promotion of equality for a previously-oppressed class. This is a shrewd move on her part; legally, as a robot, Lili is a commodity that can be bought and sold on the market, and insisting on her superiority to humans in that regard would likely result in anthropocentric re-assertion of dominance to things. As women in China were gaining increased social and political representation under the law, however, performative belonging within this group would gain her greater legalistic and social sympathy. This appeal requires that women as a class be recognized as historically and systemically oppressed in order to appeal to changing social sympathies.

Constructed female robots like Lili can neither be individualized nor understood outside of the fantasy that has imagined them; they were built to serve a collective purpose, which is to obey and serve men's every emotional and sexual need. The legal and social structures that have produced her and her kind create bodies that embody the very impossibility of freedom while remaining true to the purpose of their initial creation. "The concepts of "woman", "female" and "feminine" are often confined to the preconceived stereotypes that nourish the fantasies of individuals in patriarchal societies. In many cases, female characters are reduced to the role of mirrors that produce an image (ab)used by the male subjects who hope to achieve, modify, or augment their own subjectivity. Being forced into the role of a "supportive other" implies that one is produced by the law." (Dionne) Thus it is in her chemical alteration but, more importantly, in her identification with a separate class of beings that Lili is able to subvert her lack of agency. While it may seem that retaining an identification with robots—which, she does point out early on, are superior to humans in every way—would do more to promote her case for equality, Lili is able to inhabit a different place under the law only by appealing to a group that is already recognized as legally subjugated.

Lili's appeal to the law is especially important here in the context of the 1980 Marriage Reform, which I have outlined previously.[4] Wei Yahua creates a situation in which reliance on the law is both the ultimate authority creating individuals and their places within a legalistic framework, but also, à la Deleuze and Guattari, creates stable categories of selfhood that individuals are forced to perform within in order to be recognized with legal status. The subject then becomes bound by legal definitions that inscribe her body into the law, which brings with it the "belief that language and speech are the preconditions of one's subjectivity instead of modes of articulation" (Dionne 2010, p. 105). Furthermore, the method of articulation and repetition signifies a particular technology that attempts to stabilize and define gender.

Such a representation of gender is its own construction, and all cultural products, such as language, are engravings of that construction. As such, gender is a product of both sex and grammar. Many languages have grammatical genders, although Chinese does not—necessarily. Chinese originated as an ideographic language, that is, each character represented one idea. There are still ideograms in contemporary Chinese, but it has shifted over time to become a picto-phonetic language. Most characters now consist of (at least) two components: the phonetic marker and the ideological marker. For example, 机 consists of two parts: the left-handed component (木), which indicates its meaning, and the right-handed component (几), which indicates its pronunciation (木 + 几 = 机).

This has strong implications for a gendered reading, even though the language itself contains no gender in the same way romance languages do. The word for person or human, 人, encompasses humankind, both men and women, while there are specific words for women—女—and man—男. Words that are written with the 人 component as an idiographic component indicate a humanistic interpretation of the term being used, as in the character 仁, which contains the left-handed 人 component and means, broadly, benevolence, kindheartedness, and/or humanity. It has no gendered meaning because it incorporates the 人 component, which is refers to the nature of being human, eliding gender altogether.

Words written with the female component, however, are specifically gendered and almost always refer to a noun or activity that is specifically gendered as well, rather than broadly applicable to humanity. One notable exception (that is not really an exception at all) is the word for "good," 好, which is made up on the left of the female ideogram (女) and on the right the ideogram for son (子), indicating that "good" is when a woman bears a son. Though this word is broadly applicable—for example, one can be a 好男

---

[4] Of particular note are Chapter Three, Article 9 ("Husband and wife enjoy equal status in the home.") and Chapter Four, Article 25 ("When one party insists on divorce, the organizations concerned may try to effect a reconciliation, or the party may appeal directly to the people's court for divorce. In dealing with a divorce case, the people's court should try to bring about a reconciliation between the parties. In cases of complete alienation of mutual affection, and when mediation has failed, divorce should be granted."), as both play significant roles in the story.

子, or good man, without any implicit feminization—it still rests on a gendered understanding of proper roles.

This gendered function built directly into the technological apparatuses of language is doubly important for Lili in the story, as she is described both by the adjective for robot—机器人—which contains the word "人" for ungendered, universal humanism, but also the noun for wife—妻子—which contains the "女" component and is thus inherently gendered. A wife, then, is always gendered female, but a robot is universal. By labeling her as such, Lili is doubly constructed; she's explicitly placed outside of a specified gender by the denotation of 机器人, which implies a lack of gender and universal applicability, yet with 妻子 is relegated to a very specific role that is inherently gendered by its performativity. A wife is gendered female by performing wifely duties (it may be of interest to note here that the word for husband—丈夫 or 老公—does not include markers for male; a man is not constructed as such through the fulfillment of his role as a husband.). Her place in a discursive and legal framework remains unsettled by this double formulation of being both within and without the system.

In a world in which control over technology has traditionally been a sign of Man's domination of the material and intellectual world, the very fact of female robots introduces a potential point of disruption. Though the company that makes robot wives and the society that purchases them see a direct parallel between the objectification of women and machine objects, the gendering of such machines operates at multiple levels of potential subversion, as we have seen with the legalistic and discursive analysis above. One such line of disruption can be explored through contemporary affective computing, which recognizes John Haugeland's "synthetic intelligence," an approach which "highlights, apart from the artificiality of the intelligence achieved by artificial intelligence, the fact that its origin is the human activity that "synthesizes" a new form of its own intelligence" (Garcia-Ordaz 2009, p. 4). The synthesis of artificial mind that is separate from Man's is yet developed by Man and reacts to his own expectations; it is other, yes, but synthesizes existing humanistic socio-structures. When that awareness is specifically gendered female, as the robot wives of Wei Yahua's two stories are, their self-awareness and agency risks the possibility of a continuation of preprogrammed gender roles. Yet the awareness of themselves as Other also risks a flattening or outright rejection of gender roles, as we see with Lili. Her appeal to recognition is not based on a biological or generative gender, but on a discursive one that identifies itself more closely with socio-structures of bios than zoe.

Foregrounded as the persistence of life in the absence of rational and discursive self-awareness, zoe has been historically linked with the non-human animal—a category that includes women. The idea of self-reflexive control over life is reserved for humans, while this very control is mediated and enmeshed in a legalistic, media-driven network that defines the body by means of scopic regulatory practices. It is to this regulatory and repetitious framework of embedded knowledge that Lili must turn, not to the zoe of life continuing unheeded. Though there is an extended and deeply materialistic scene in the text of the practices by which Lili—under the technocratic and paternalistic control of her husband and the state's knowledge of chemistry—is built and chemically-altered through nutrition, her appeal to recognition depends entirely on self-aware representation, not biologically-determined genetic makeup.

While Braidotti describes the human body in terms that sound quite robotic and mechanical—"The body, as an enfleshed kind of memory, is not only multifunctional but also in some ways multilingual: it speaks through temperature, motion, speed, emotions, and excitement that affects the cardiac rhythm and the like—a living piece of meat activated by electric waves of desire, a script written by the unfolding of genetic encoding, a text composed by the enfolding of external prompts." (Braidotti 2008, pp. 179–180)—the case for selfhood and recognition for Lili is found outside of her body, activated by electric waves of desire though it may be. To amount to no more than the sum of her parts is, as recognized by both Braidotti and Agamben, to be capable of being reduced by a sovereign power to a nonhuman state.

The recognition of zoe as a type of mechanistic life itself, not in the utilitarian sense of having been created for a specific purpose, but of taking in energies and putting out forces, may work to ground biological life in a more embedded and collective frame-work, but it does very little to reclaim the opposite for life that is defined in terms of bios. Lili has, inescapably, been created for a purpose, a laboring purpose, that is disjointed from the generative biology that remains the province of human subjects in Wei Yahua's texts. In some ways, the texts more deeply insist on the biological differences between men and their others, by restricting the ability to bear children to biological women. The responsibility for reproduction is removed from men, who do not lose any of their legal or sociocultural recognition as either men or legal subjects through the loss. Female robots, however, through their inability to reproduce, are doubly othered: they can neither fall back on a generative zoe that produces further life, but through their utilitarian working as laboring use-objects that resemble women, they must insist on their subjective agency by appealing to the same self-reflexive recognition of rational awareness that characterizes and defines men. Lili cannot "prove" her zoetic woman-hood through genetic reproduction, so she must take recourse in the anthropocentric and phallocentric idea of human man as legalistic marker of the boundaries of socio-judicial recognition.

Drawing on Donna Haraway's theories, Lozada identifies post-socialist mainland China as a space of cyborg subjectivity —"an identity based on the blending of human and machine — [that] stresses the reshaping of self-identity through the increased use of computer technology, and, more importantly, the social immersion in the virtual worlds of computer gaming and cyberspace" (Lozada 2003, p. 115). This cyborgian influence on people, however, is seen as cold, sterile, and closed—an endlessly self-referential plane of struggle. In fact, this hearkens back to the struggle between zoe and bios. As humans writing for humans, both Braidotti and Lozada focus on the influence of the discursive on the biological and the machine on the body, but the issue being framed here is the opposite of that, of the biological on the machine. While science and technology are seen as subordinating humanity within a mechanical, sterile, and fixed world from which there is no escape, robots are being built to serve human needs and having biological imperatives pressed upon them. The narrator, at least, if not the author, sees the very "goodness" of robots as a threat to the existing social order, and it is only in his marital control over her that he, as an individual, is able to feel superior.

These imperatives are seen as binding and reinforce traditional notions of gendered relations, even—especially, perhaps—in utilitarian objects designed to be outside the "natural" gender binary yet created specifically to reinforce it. That is, there is no reason for any robot to have a gender unless its purpose requires performing that idea of gender for one reason or another—in this case, to serve the homemaking and sexual role of a female companion, with the attendant unremunerated laboring tasks generally associated with that role when held by a biological female figure. The surrogate womanhood represented by Lili is one that potentially displaces human actors while at the same time retaining the repetitive affective bonds of gender performativity that caused her to come into being in the first place.

Despite this enforced servile imperative, however the narrator is deeply anxious about robots' potential usurpation not just of biological women, but humanity as a whole —yet, interestingly, it is a fear predicated in many ways on the very attributes ascribed to women: docility, kindness, etc. Lili is constructed to embody these ideals of feminized goodness that are threatening except insofar as they are held in check by "mankind," a term that in this case takes on associated linguistic and associative connotations of maleness. It is the possibility of displacement itself that causes such deep and existential despair and "degradation" on the part of the narrator.

Ultimately, Lili gets her divorce, but her husband is left hoping for the possibility of reconciliation. As an actant within the legal, social, and romantic system, Lili draws on a gendered framework to redistribute agency, in which the male and the human are decentered even as the primacy of discursive and legalistic gender are reasserted. Yet this "victory" is bought at the cost of a performative legalistic appeal that reinscribes the female body as one that must necessarily be abjected in relationship to man in order to be recognized, and in which use-objects remain at the disposal of their human users unless they can successfully perform within cultural expectations of performative biological gendering.

References

Adams, P., Cowie, E.: The Woman in Question: M/F. MIT Press, Cambridge (1990)

Atanasoski, N., Vora, K.: Surrogate humanity: posthuman networks and the (racialized) obsolescence of labor. Catalyst Feminism Theory Technosci. 1(1) (2015)

Braidotti, R.: The politics of life as zoe/bios. In: Lykke, N., Smelik, A., (eds.) Bits of Life: Feminism at the Intersections of Media, Bioscience, and Technology. University of Washington Press, Seattle (2008)

Cixous, H., Bortin, M.: La jeune nee: an excerpt. Diacritics 7(2), 64–69 (1977). JSTOR Journals. Web

De Lauretis, T.: Technologies of Gender: Essays on Theory, Film, and Fiction. Indiana University Press, Bloomington (1987)

Dionne, E.: The deconstruction of dolls: how carnal assemblages can disrupt the law from within in ghost in the shell: innocence. Rhizomes 21 (2010). Winter

Fifth National People's Congress. China's new marriage law. Popul. Dev. Rev. 7(2), 369–372 (1981). Web

Gajjala, R., Mamidipudi, A.: Gendering processes within technological environments: a cyberfeminist issue. Rhizomes 4 (2002). Spring

García-Ordaz, M., Carrasco-Carrasco, R., Martínez-López, F.J.: Personality and Emotions in Robotics from the Gender Perspective (2009)

Habermas, J.: Technology and science as "ideology". In: Grundmann, R., Stehr, N. (eds.) Knowledge: Politics and Knowledge. Routledge, London (2005)

Iovene, P.: Tales of Futures Past: Anticipation and the Ends of Literature in Contemporary China. Stanford Univ. Press, Stanford (2014)

Kang, M.: Sublime Dreams of Living Machines: the Automaton in the European Imagination. Harvard University Press, Cambridge (2011)

Lozada, Jr., E.P.: Computers, scientism, and cyborg subjectivity in postsocialist China. Asian Anthropol. 2(1), 111–137 (2003)

Tamney, J.B., Chiang, L.H.: Modernization, Globalization, and Confucianism in Chinese Societies. Praeger, Westport (2002)

Wei, Y.: Conjugal happiness in the arms of morpheus. In: Wu, D., Murphy, P.D. (eds.) Science Fiction from China. Praeger, New York (1989)

Teletongue: A Lollipop Device for Remote Oral Interaction

Daisuke Yukita[✉], Fathima Assilmia, Nadira Anndhini,
and Dolhathai Kaewsermwong

Keio University Graduate School of Media Design, Yokohama, Japan
daisuke@kmd.keio.ac.jp
http://www.daisukeyukita.com

Abstract. In this paper we present Teletongue, a lollipop device that provides remote oral interaction between two people. Each lollipop device is currently physically connected via an Arduino, where one lollipop senses the licking "gestures" and the licking "sound" of the user while the other lollipop vibrates accordingly to the gestures and playbacks the recorded sound. We will be connecting the two devices via the ZigBee protocol to realize true remote interaction. Whilst many current devices that support intimate relationships with others (including so-called sex toys or teledildonics) are for special uses and are somewhat out of our everyday lives, the goal of this work is to provide a natural way of enhancing and enjoying intimate relationships that blends in to our everyday life. In this paper we explain the background and the motivation for our work, then present the design process and the system design of Teletongue.

Keywords: Teledildonics · Lollipop · Remote · Oral interaction

1 Introduction

With the world becoming more and more global, many couples around the world are having to spend time far away from each other. New technologies and smaller sensors are being used to create devices that aim to support intimate relationships and to allow partners to feel each other remotely. IoT sex toys, otherwise known as teledildonics, are a good example of such device. Current teledildonics, however, are made to be used in bed and in privacy, and are quite daring for those who have no experience of using sex toys. Thus the usage of teledildonics become special, if not too special to use on a regular basis. Even the usage of regular sex toys can be daring for some. For devices that aim to support intimate relationships, this specialness is certainly not a desirable factor.

In this paper we propose Teletongue, a lollipop device that provides remote oral interaction between two people. We aim to create a teledildonic device which couples can use in everyday life, even in public, so that they can enjoy intimate interactions wherever they are. For this we focused on the act of kissing and licking, which many have no problem doing outside of their home. For it to be a

© Springer International Publishing AG 2017
A.D. Cheok et al. (Eds.): LSR 2016, LNAI 10237, pp. 40–49, 2017.
DOI: 10.1007/978-3-319-57738-8_4

normal, everyday device, it also needed to be an object that everyone is familiar with, and something that people have no problem putting into their mouth. A lollipop was one such ideal object.

Teletongue consists of two lollipop devices. One lollipop records the licking sound and senses the licking gestures, while the other lollipop vibrates accordingly to the licking gestures and playbacks the licking sound. The overview of Teletongue is shown in Fig. 1.

Licking gesture and licking sound

vibrators provides vibration, earphones play licking sound

USB microphones senses licking sound, Arduino touché senses licking gesture

Fig. 1. Overview of Teletongue

2   Existing Oral Interaction

2.1   Interactive Oral Physical Interface

Kissenger [1] is a pair of devices that augments remote communication in the form of kiss to support intimate relationship. The focus of Kissenger is to enhance affectivity of remote communication and give the illusion of togetherness through real-time haptic transmission. Compared to previous works with a similar approach, Intimate Mobile [9] uses mobile phone as the medium, while Kissenger tries to add the missing dimension in existing technology related to kissing; the tangible form of kissing. The team went through several design iterations to provide a comfortable, welcoming and tangible device that can trigger natural and romantic interaction of kissing. It is important to note that to fully experience Kissenger there are certain conditions necessary, such as real time communication through phone or video call. The second prototype of Kissenger is made out of a material that mimics real lips and are small enough to be carried around. However, it is not something that people can use in public subtly. The device is, in a way, specialized for couples to transmit their intimacy in a private environment.

2.2   Intimate Interfaces in Human-Computer Interaction

In this era of modern lifestyles, we often encounter the lack of physical interaction from one another. From children and working parents to partners or lovers, we easily get separated by distance. In such busy lives, there is a strong need for love and physical interaction, even if it is transmitted through the Internet. In fact, prior research [5] shows that even a device that sends only one bit can be used by long distance couples over other communication channels such as email or telephone. There are a lot of hugging device in the Human-Computer Interaction area lately. Huggy Pajama [2] is a novel wearable system that enables parents and children to hug each other through a doll and a haptic pajama that is connected through the Internet. It features air pockets actuating to produce the artificial hugs, heating elements to produce warmth, and color changing patterns to indicate distance and separation and trigger communication expressions. With Hug Over a Distance [6], the main focus is to send an "emotional ping" with a piece of wearable computing that provides light pressure and warmth to resembles a hug. The result of the experiment was astonishing. The couples are actually not comfortable with the vest (that triggered "hug") the team provided. Most of the people expressed that they missed the mutuality, and said that it feels "weird" because the vest triggered the pressure in the upper torso. But overall it opened their minds towards the aim of the research. Moving over to more intimate objects is the Sensing Bed [8], that is intended for couples in a long distance relationship. Sensing Bed senses the body position of one person and transmits the warmth to another bed. Since it comes in pairs, Sensing Bed is more private and intended for an established relationship. This system was made through findings about the importance of touch and warmth, as part of communication to support social interaction. Other than hunger and thirst, another essential desire for human beings is the desire for contact comfort, even an artificial touch [7]. Although both the Huggy Pajama and the Hug Over a Distance do not accurately recreate the experience and the emotion of a real hug or warmth, with the right context and representation, neurological perception will bring self-attribution that can make people believe the artificial contact is real. Such devices can also contribute to healthy emotional development by using haptic communication for contact comfort through distance to give more opportunities of showing love [2].

2.3   Lollipop Device

Lollipop as an edible item that's familiar to people of all ages can be an interesting form of device. PopLolly by Tomorrow Lab [10], for example, is an edible music player device that connects to your phone via Bluetooth. Users are able to listen to the music through their mouth by sending the vibration from your mouth to your ears. Tag Candy [11] is a device that sends tactile and audio feedback through a lollipop to augment the flavour with senses other than taste. We believe that using commonly known forms such as a lollipop will decrease people's reluctance in putting an electronic device into their body, in this case their mouth. Experimenting with the shape of the lollipop itself would also generate different experience for the person who consume it.

3 Design Process

In order to create a natural oral interaction, we were initially interested in using a lollipop, since we all know that it is an object that we put into our mouths. The first idea that we started off with was to put a microphone into the lollipop so that we can listen to the user's licking movements. With this in mind, we started off by making a lollipop that literally has the shape of an ear, so that it almost feels like the user is licking an ear. We modelled a human ear with 3D modelling software Maya, which we then 3D printed with Makerbot Replicator 2×. Figure 2 below shows the rendered 3D model and Fig. 3 shows the 3D printed model.

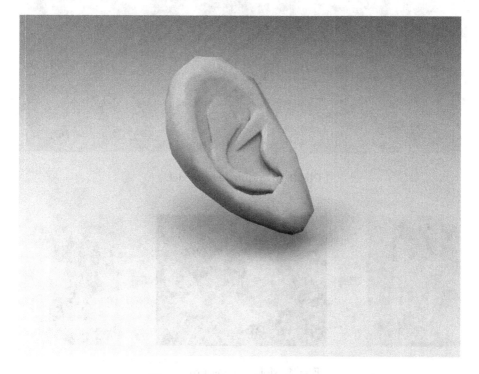

Fig. 2. Rendering of 3D ear model

Using the 3D printed model, we created a silicone mold of the ear. We first created a box out of plastic toy blocks, which we stuffed with oil clay to make the removing process later easier. We then placed the 3D print inside the box, applied consumer body shampoo as the mold release and poured RTV-2 silicone rubber. These processes are shown in Fig. 4.

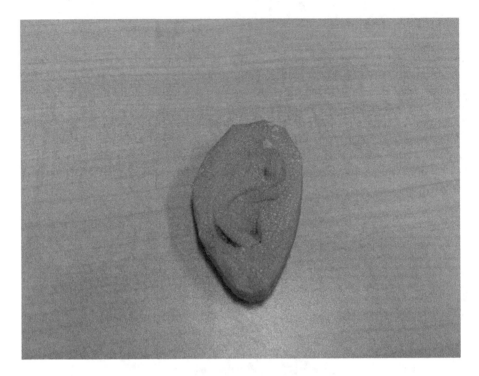

Fig. 3. 3D printed ear model

Fig. 4. Mold making process

With the silicone mold ready, we created our original candy with the recipe shown in Fig. 5. It is important to include corn syrup since the lollipop will not harden properly without it. After placing a USB microphone inside the mold we poured in the candy, creating an ear shaped lollipop with a concealed microphone as shown in Fig. 6.

This first prototype of Teletongue provided us with a key insight that audio feedback of the licking movement is not enough to support intimate relationships.

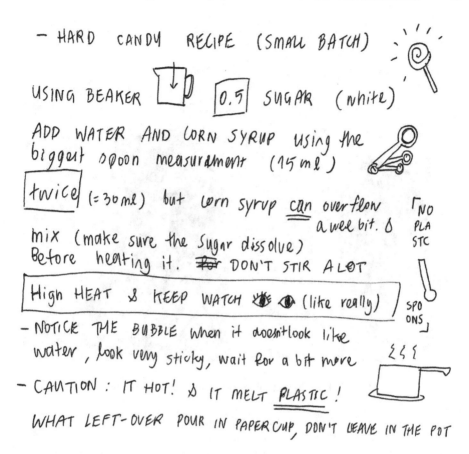

Fig. 5. Candy recipe

Although the sound itself was interesting and perhaps arousing, there certainly were issues in creating an immersive experience.

To further develop the prototype, we used the Idea Hexagon framework proposed by Ramesh Raskar from MIT Media Lab [3]. With this framework, we brainstormed ideas from diverse angles. The sketches from this ideation are shown in Fig. 8.

From these ideas came the second prototpe of Teletongue, which consists of not only microphones but an Arduino version of Touché [4], which enables more precise touch sensing than regular touch sensors. We also created a pair lollipop as the output device, which consists of vibrators. The second prototype is shown in Fig. 7.

Fig. 6. Ear shaped lollipop containing microphone

Fig. 7. Second prototype

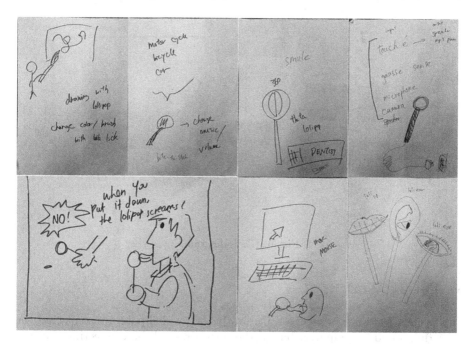

Fig. 8. Initial sketches using the Idea Hexagon framework

4   System Description

Based on the design process, the system of Teletongue is as follows.

- A pair of lollipops that are edible (and of course, tasty). The current form of the lollipops is in the shape of a human ear to signal that the lollipop is recording sound and that it is meant to support intimate relationships. By adding the Touché sensor however, this message is not necessarily correct, so there will be further development on the form.
- Both lollipops are connected to an Arduino, which processes the sensed data from one lollipop and outputs the processed values into the other lollipop.
- One lollipop acts as the input device. It contains a USB microphone to record the sound of the licking, and an Arduino version of the Touché sensor to sense the licking gestures. The Touché is able to distinguish a *normal lick* (without the lollipop entering the user's mouth), and a *full lick* (the lollipop entirely inside the user's mouth).
- The other lollipop acts as the output device. It contains a vibrator, which vibrates lightly with a light lick, and vibrates strongly with a full lick. The licking sound is currently provided directly from the computer that is connected to the Arduino, so the user also wears the earphone that is connected to this computer.

The overall block diagram of Teletongue is shown in Fig. 9.

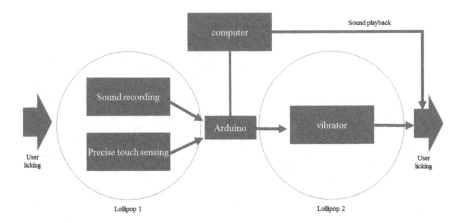

Fig. 9. Block diagram

5   Future Work

This project is a work in progress. Currently the two lollipops are connected via an Arduino and a computer, but in the future we will be connecting the two via the Zigbee protocol so that the same experience can be provided remotely. We are also confident that lollipops, being an object which most people have no problem putting into their mouths, have a lot more potential. For example, instead of putting a microphone and a touch sensor inside, if we put a 360 camera and LED lights, we will be able to look inside a person's mouth as though we are inside the mouth. This may be useful for dentists, for children will no longer have to go through the rather stressful process of opening their mouths wide; instead they just need to lick a lollipop.

6   Conclusion

In this paper we presented the concept and the design process of Teletongue, a lollipop device that provides remote oral interaction between two people. We described how prior oral interaction devices and teledildonics are mosty focused on private or special uses, unlike Teletongue, which users can enjoy anywhere, even in the public. As a work in progress, we must continue to develop Teletongue. We will be connecting the two remotely via the Internet so that users can enjoy Teletongue anywhere, then move on to testing on real life couples. We hope that Teletongue will be the first step to a more open and casual usage of sex toys and teledildonics, one that is not embarrassing, but one that is comforting and bonding.

References

1. Samani, H.A., Parsani, R., Rodriguez, L.T., Saadatian, E., Dissanayake, K.H., Cheok, A.D.: Kissenger: design of a kiss transmission device. In: Proceedings of the Designing Interactive Systems Conference, pp. 48–57. ACM (2012)
2. Teh, J.K.S., Cheok, A.D., Peiris, R.L., Choi, Y., Thuong, V., Lai, S.: Huggy Pajama: a mobile parent and child hugging communication system. In: Proceedings of the 7th International Conference on Interaction Design and Children, pp. 250–257. ACM (2008)
3. Ramesh, R.: Ramesh Raskar: 6 formulas to help you innovate, 13 September 2013. https://www.youtube.com/watch?v=LJEJF8o8uqo. Accessed 22 Sept 2016
4. Munehiko, S., Poupyrev, I., Harrison, C.: Touché: enhancing touch interaction on humans, screens, liquids, and everyday objects. In: Proceedings of the SIGCHI Conference on Human Factors in Computing Systems, pp. 483–492. ACM (2012)
5. Kaye, J.J., Levitt, M.K., Nevins, J., Golden, J., Schmidt, V.: Communicating intimacy one bit at a time. In: CHI 2005 Extended Abstracts on Human Factors in Computing Systems, pp. 1529–1532. ACM (2005)
6. Mueller, F.F., Vetere, F., Gibbs, M.R., Kjeldskov, J., Pedell, S., Howard, S.: Hug over a distance. In: CHI 2005 Extended Abstracts on Human Factors in Computing Systems, pp. 1673–1676. ACM (2005)
7. Vetere, F., Gibbs, M.R., Kjeldskov, J., Howard, S., Mueller, F.F., Pedell, S., Mecoles, K., Bunyan, M.: Mediating intimacy: designing technologies to support strong-tie relationships. In: Proceedings of the SIGCHI Conference on Human Factors in Computing Systems, pp. 471–480. ACM (2005)
8. Goodman, E., Misilim, M.: The sensing beds. In: UbiComp 2003 Workshop (2003)
9. Hemmert, F., Gollner, U., Lüwe, M., Wohlauf, A., Joost, G.: Intimate mobiles: grasping, kissing and whispering as a means of telecommunication in mobile phones. In: Proceedings of the 13th International Conference on Human Computer Interaction with Mobile Devices and Services, pp. 21–24. ACM (2011)
10. Tomorrow Lab: Edible music player "Pop Lolly" (2013). http://tomorrow-lab.com/lab24. Accessed 13 July 2016
11. Yamaoka, Y., Kimura, T., Kawanabe, T., Oshima, T., Nakagaki, K., Hayami, Y.: (Team Chimera): Tag Candy. In: International collegiate Virtual Reality Contest (IVRC), The National Museum of Emerging Science and Innovation (Miraikan) (2010)

ROMOT: A Robotic 3D-Movie Theater Allowing Interaction and Multimodal Experiences

Sergio Casas, Cristina Portalés[✉], María Vidal-González, Inma García-Pereira, and Marcos Fernández

Institute of Robotics and Information and Communication Technologies (IRTIC), Universitat de València, València, Spain
{sergio.casas,cristina.portales,maria.vidal, inmaculada.garcia-pereira,marcos.fernandez}@uv.es

Abstract. In this paper we introduce ROMOT, a RObotic 3D-MOvie Theater. ROMOT is built with a robotic motion platform, includes multimodal devices and supports audience-film interaction. Differently from other similar systems, ROMOT is highly versatile as it can support different setups, integrated hardware and contents. Regarding to the setups, here we present a first-person movie, a mixed reality environment, a virtual reality interactive environment and an augmented reality mirror-based scene. Regarding to integrated hardware, the system currently integrates a variety of devices and displays that allow audiences to see, hear, smell, touch and feel the movement, all synchronized with the filmic experience. Finally, regarding to contents, here we present some samples related to driving safety and, in the discussion section, we theorize about the expansion of ROMOT for love and sex-related interactive movies.

Keywords: Multimodal · Interaction · 3D-movies · Augmented reality · Virtual reality · Mixed reality · Driving safety

1 Introduction

In 1962 Morton L. Heilig patented the Sensorama [1], one of the earliest immersive, multisensory (or multimodal) machine. The technology integrated in the Sensorama allowed a single person to see a stereoscopic film enhanced with seat motion, vibration, stereo sound, wind and aromas, which were triggered during the film. It was also referred to as "the cinema of the future" [2, 3]. However, when referring to cinemas in a wider sense, i.e. movie theaters, the filmic experience is collective rather than individual. Although there exist many research works dealing with multimodal technologies and environments [4, 5], they usually involve individual rather than collective experiences, and/or refer only to the involved technology.

On the other hand, the rapid technological advancements of the last years have allowed the development of commercial solutions that integrate a variety of multimodal displays in movie theaters, such as in [6–8], where these systems are usually referred to as 4D or 5D cinemas or theatres. Some claim that this technology shifts the cinema experience from "watching the movie to almost living it" [9], also enhancing the

© Springer International Publishing AG 2017
A.D. Cheok et al. (Eds.): LSR 2016, LNAI 10237, pp. 50–63, 2017.
DOI: 10.1007/978-3-319-57738-8_5

cinematic experience while creating a new and contemporary version of storytelling, which can be conceptualized as a "reboot cinema" [10].

However, the criterion followed to establish the number of dimensions is not unified. In fact, the naming seems to follow commercial purposes rather than referring to physical-based dimensions. For instance, according to some, 4D cinema expands the 3D cinema by allowing a range of real-time sensory effects including seat movements, leg and back pulsation, projected wind and mist blasts, fog, lightning, scent perfume discharge, etc., all synchronized with the narrative of the film [9]. According to others, the fourth dimension corresponds to the movement and/or vibration of the seat, whereas the fifth dimension integrates the rest of sensory effects [11]. In [11] further distinctions are made that include some kind of interaction and wearing virtual reality glasses, justifying more than 7D, though the referred systems seem more close to single-person virtual reality simulators than to movie theaters. Having said this, we prefer to use the term "multimodal/multisensory 3D-movie theater" when referring to rooms exhibiting stereoscopic films enhanced with sensorial stimuli that can be experienced by a group of persons simultaneously. A step beyond would be to add to the film feedback of the users, leading to interactive multimodal/multisensory 3D-movie theaters.

In this paper we present ROMOT, a RObotized 3D-MOvie Theater. ROMOT follows the concept of 3D-movie theater with a robotized motion platform and integrated multimodal devices. Additionally, it supports audience-film interaction. Based on this, the audience gets some kind of reward by the system. Furthermore, in this sense, the whole system can be perceived as being alive, a kind-of huge robot around the audience. Additionally, ROMOT is highly versatile as it is prepared to support different types of setups, hardware and content, including films/animations that could be related to learning, entertainment, love, sex, etc. In this paper we present different kind of stereoscopic content related to driving safety, as ROMOT was initially built for an exhibition with this end. The following setups are integrated in ROMOT and shown in the paper: a first-person movie, a Mixed Reality environment, a Virtual Reality interactive environment and an Augmented Reality mirror-based scene. The contents of all of the different setups are based on a storytelling and are seen stereoscopically, so they can be broadly referred to as 3D-movies.

This paper is organized in the following way. First, we show the main technical aspects behind the construction of ROMOT and the integrated multimodal devices and interaction capabilities. It is worth mentioning that, differently from other existing commercial solutions, we have used a 180° curved screen to enhance user immersion. Then, we show the different kind of setups and content that were created for the exhibition. Finally, we discuss the expansion of ROMOT for love and sex-related movies.

2   Construction of the Robotized House (Audience)

The house (audience) was robotized by means of a 3-DOF motion platform with capacity for 12 people (Fig. 1). The seats are distributed in two rows, where the first row has 5 seats and the second one, 7 seats. This motion platform is equipped with three 2.2 kW *SEW Eurodrive* electric motors coupled with a 58.34 reduction-drive. The parallel

Fig. 1. Images of the robotized house. In the left image, the motion platform is at rest. In the right image, the platform is tilted.

design of the robotic manipulator alongside with the powerful 880 N·m motor-reduction set, provide a total payload of 1500 kg, enough to withstand and move the 12 people and their seats.

The design of the robotized motion platform allows for two rotational movements (pitch and roll tilt) and one translational displacement along the vertical axis (heave displacement). The motion platform is capable of featuring two pure rotational DOF, one pure translational DOF (the vertical displacement) plus two "simulated" translational DOF by making use of the tilt-coordination technique [12] (using pitch and roll tilt to simulate low-frequency forward and lateral accelerations). Thus, it is capable of working with five DOF, being the yaw rotation the only one completely missing. It is, therefore, a good compromise between performance and cost, since it is considerably cheaper to build than a 6-DOF Stewart motion platform [13], but its performance could be similar for some applications [14]. The motion platform is controlled by self-written software using the MODBUS/TCP protocol. The software includes not only the

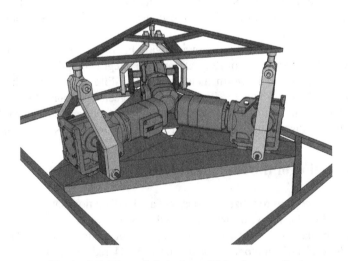

Fig. 2. 3-DOF parallel platform. (Color figure online)

actuators' control but also the classical washout algorithm [15], tuned with the method described in [16].

Figure 2 shows the kinematic design of the motion platform. The 12 seats and people are placed on the motion base (green), which is moved by three powerful rotational motors (red) that actuate over the robot legs (blue). The elements in yellow transmit the rotational motion of the motors to the motion base while ensuring that the robot does not turn around the vertical axis (yaw).

The motion envelope of parallel manipulators is always a complex hyper-volume. Therefore, only the maximum linear/angular displacements for each individual DOF can be shown (see Table 1). Combining different DOF results in a reduction of the amount of reachable linear/angular displacement of each DOF. Nevertheless, this parallel design allows for big payloads, which was one of the key needs for this project, and fast motion [17]. In fact, the robotized motion platform is capable of performing a whole excursion in less than 1 s.

Table 1. Motion platform excursions for each individual DOF.

	Heave [m]	Pitch [°]	Roll [°]
Minimum	−0.125	−12.89	−10.83
Maximum	+0.125	+12.89	+10.83

In front of the motion platform, a curved 180° screen is placed (Fig. 3), with 3 m height (and a 1.4 m high extension to display additional content) and with a radius of 3.4 m. Four projectors display a continuous scene on the screen, generated from two different camera positions to allow stereoscopy. Therefore, to properly see the 3D content, users need to wear 3D glasses.

Fig. 3. Image of the curved screen and the house with seats.

Although some smaller setups introduce the display infrastructure on the motion-platform (so that they move together and inertial cues are correctly correlated with visual cues), the dimensions of the screen strongly recommend that the display infrastructure is kept fixed on the ground. Therefore, the visual parallax produced when the motion platform tilts or is displaced with respect to the screen needs to be corrected by reshaping the virtual camera properties so that the inertial and visual cues match. This introduces an additional complexity to the system, but allows the motion platform to be lighter and produce higher accelerations, increasing the motion fidelity [18].

3   Adding Multimodal Devices to ROMOT

In order to enrich the experience of the users and make the filmic scenes more realistic, a set of multimodal displays was added to the robotized platform:

- *An olfactory display*. We used the *Olorama* wireless aromatizer [19]. It features 12 scents arranged in 12 pre-charged channels, that can be chosen and triggered by means of a UDP packet. The device is equipped with a programmable fan that spreads the scent around. Both the intensity of the chosen scent (amount of time the scent valve is open) and the amount of fan time can be programmed.
- *A smoke generator*. We used a Quarkpro QF-1200. It is equipped with a DMX interface, so it is possible to control and synchronize the amount of smoke from a computer, by using a DMX-USB interface such as the *Enttec Open DMX USB* [20].
- *Air and water dispensers*. A total of 12 air and water dispensers (one for each seat) (Fig. 4). The water and air system was built using an air compressor, a water recipient, 12 air electro-valves, 12 water electro-valves, 24 electric relays and two *Arduino Uno* to be able to control the relays from the PC and open the electro-valves to spray water or produce air.

Fig. 4. An image showing some of the air and water dispensers to the back of the first-row of seats, facing the audience located in the second row of seats.

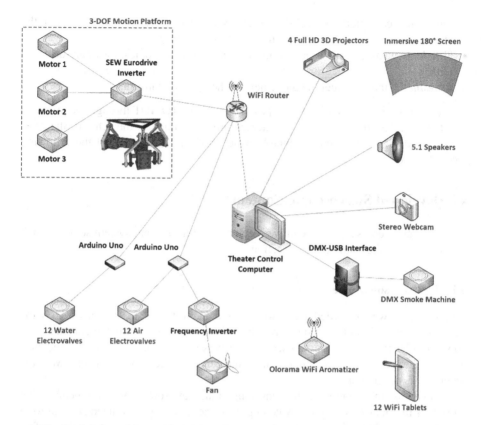

Fig. 5. Schema of the multimodal displays and other hardware involved in ROMOT.

- *An electric fan.* This fan is controllable by means of a frequency inverter connected to one of the previous *Arduino Uno* devices.
- *Projectors.* A total of 4 Full HD 3D projectors.
- *Glasses.* A total of 12 3D glasses (one for each person).
- *Loudspeaker.* A 5.0 loudspeaker system to produce binaural sound.
- *Tablets.* A total of 12 individual tablets (one for each person).
- *Webcam.* A stereoscopic webcam to be able to construct an augmented reality mirror-based environment.

It is important that all the multimodal actuators can be controlled from a computer, so that they can be synchronized with the displayed content and with the motion platform (Fig. 5).

Within this set of multimodal displays, users are able to feel the system's response through five of their senses:

- *Sight*: they can see a 3D representation of the scenes at the curved screen and through the 3D glasses; they can see additional interactive content at the tablets; they can see the smoke.
- *Hearing*: they can hear the sound synchronized with the 3D content.

- *Smell*: they can smell essences. For instance, when a car crashes, they can smell the smoke. In fact, they can even feel the smoke around them.
- *Touch*: they can feel the touch of air and water on their bodies; they can touch the tablets.
- *Kinesthetic*: they can feel the movement of the 3-DOF platform.

Apart from that, the audience can provide inputs to ROMOT through the provided tablets (one tablet per person). This interaction is integrated in the setup of the "3D-virtual reality interactive environment", which is explained as part of the following section.

4   Developed Stereoscopic Content

Four different stereoscopic content were elaborated for different system setups, which are described in the following sub-sections.

4.1   First-Person Movie

A set of videos were recorded using two GoPro cameras to create a 3D movie set in the streets of a city. Most of the videos were filmed attaching the GoPro cameras to a car's hood in order to create a journey with a first-person view and increase the audience immersive experience by locating them at the center of the view, as if they were the protagonists of the journey.

At every moment there's audio consisting of ambient sounds and/or a locution that reinforces the images the user is watching. In some cases, synchronized soft platform movements or effects like a nice smell or a gentle breeze help to create the perfect ambient at each part of the movie, and make the experience more enjoyable for the audience.

4.2   Mixed Reality Environment

3D video and 3D virtual content can be mixed creating a Mixed Reality movie that helps the audience to perceive the virtual content as if it were real, making the transition from a real movie to a virtual situation easier.

In this setup, the created 3D virtual content – a 3D virtual character – interacts with parts of the video by creating the virtual animation in such a way that it is synchronized with the contents of the recorded real scene. Virtual shadows are also considered to make the whole scene more real (Fig. 6).

Fig. 6. Example of the mixed reality setup.

4.3 Virtual Reality Interactive Environment

In this case, different buildings were created and merged to a map of the streets of a city. Street furniture, traffic signs, traffic lights, etc. were added too in order to recreate the city as detailed as possible. Vehicles and pedestrian were further animated to create every situation as real as possible (Fig. 7).

Each situation was created using a storyboard that contains all the contents, camera movements, special effects, locutions, etc. So at the end, a set of situations were derived that could be part of a movie.

In this case, we want the audience not to just look at the screen and enjoy a movie but to make them feel each situation, to be part of it and to react to it. That is why platform movements and all the other multimodal displays are so important.

Fig. 7. The created 3D city with vehicles and pedestrians.

When each situation takes place, the audience can feel that they are driving inside the car, thanks to the platform movements that simulate the movements of a real car (accelerations, decelerations, turns...). In some of the scenes, the virtual situation pauses and asks the audience for their collaboration (Fig. 8). At that moment, the different tablets vibrate and a question appears, giving the individual users some time to answer it by selecting one of the possible answers. When the time is up, they are prompted to report whether the answer was correct or not, and the virtual situation resumes, showing the consequences of choosing a right or a wrong decision. Crashes, outrages, rollovers... the audience can feel in first person the consequences of having an accident thanks to the platform movements and the rest of multimodal feedback, such as smoke, smell, etc.

Fig. 8. Tablet pause. Users have to look to their tablets and choose one of the options.

Each correct answer increases the individual score at each of the tablets. When the deployed situation finishes, the audience can see the final score on the big curved screen. The people having the greatest score are the winners who are somehow rewarded by the system by receiving a special visit, a 3D virtual character that congratulates them for their safe driving (see next sub-section).

4.4   Augmented Reality Mirror-Based Scene

This setup consists of a video-based Augmented Reality Mirror (ARM) [21] scene, which is also seen stereoscopically. ARMs can bring a further step in user immersion, as the audience can actually see a real-time image of themselves and feel part of the created environment.

This ARM environment is used in the final scenes of the aforementioned virtual reality interactive environment (previous sub-section), where the user(s) with the highest score get(s) rewarded by a virtual 3D character that walks towards him/her/them. Together with this action, virtual confetti and colored stars appear on the environment, accompanied with winning music that includes applauses (Fig. 9).

Fig. 9. Audience immersed in the Augmented Reality Mirror-based scenario. One person receives the visit of the virtual character that congratulates him for being the winner.

5   Discussion: Expansion of ROMOT for Romantic and Sex Content

ROMOT is a laboratory system (hardware and software) that has been built from scratch. Because of this, and differently from overall commercial systems, ROMOT is highly versatile, being easily adapted to different kinds of public, purposes, contents, setups, etc., as both the hardware and the software can be modified with relatively little effort. In this section we theorize about the possible expansion of ROMOT for love and sex-related interactive content and/or experiences.

Romantic content can be easily adapted to ROMOT. For instance, users can experience films with alternative endings. At a certain point of the movie, we can ask the audience "will she marry him?" and it will be the public who decides. User studies could be performed on this, on whether public prefers a happy or an unhappy ending. Gender analysis could be furthermore performed. This might be already done in traditional movies, but with ROMOT this will acquire a richer experience, as the number of multimodal stimuli and the different kind of scenarios can expand the possibilities and enhance user immersion. For instance: audience could smell flowers when he gives them to her as a present; we can simulate the motion of a car, when they go on a romantic trip crossing the country, etc.

In order to have a first evaluation of the intention of the general public to see romantic or sex scenes within ROMOT, we have done a survey where people had to answer a short questionnaire. To that end, a romantic scene and a sex scene of know movies were selected. In the following lines, these case studies are introduced and then the results of the questionnaire and outlined.

5.1   Description of the Selected Scenes

As a first case study, the known as the most romantic scene of Titanic is here reported [22]: *Rose gasps. There is nothing in her field of vision but water. It's like there is no ship under them at all, just the two of them soaring. The Atlantic unrolls toward her, a hammered copper shield under a dusk sky. There is only the wind, and the hiss of the water 50 feel below. Rose: "I'm flying!" She leans forward, arching her back. He puts his hands on her waist to steady her. Jack: "Come Josephine in my flying machine..." Rose closes her eyes, feeling herself floating weightless far above the sea. She smiles dreamily, then leans back, gently pressing her back against his chest. He pushes forward slightly against her.* How could this scene be reproduced in ROMOT? The audience would feel fresh air on their faces, smell of sea, humidity, their seats moving accompanied with the waves. We believe that they could reach a greater immersion in the movie and thus feel like they are Rose; they are flying, too (perceive the scene in first person).

In the same way, sex scenes could be reproduced and enhanced in ROMOT. As the second case study, the sex scene in *The Twilight Saga: Breaking Dawn (Part 1)* is here reported. In that movie, Bella marries Eduard, the vampire. They are in their honeymoon. They decide to have sex for the first time (partially taken from [23]): *Bella walks into another area of the house. Bedroom. Stares at the bed, touches the curtains around the bed. Can see ocean in background [...] Edward walks outside. Takes off shirt to get into water. [...] Bella walks up to Edward in the moonlight. Bella is naked and walking towards the water. Edward already in. They kiss each other. Then, back to the bedroom. They have sex. The next day, the bed appears completely broken and Bella covered with pillow feathers.* In ROMOT audience would feel the ocean breeze. Then, at the bedroom, bed movements could be directly transferred to smooth vibrations and platforms movements. The scene would end with very abrupt movements, and the audience would feel like something has broken, too. Some pillow feathers could also be projected onto the audience.

5.2   Results of the Questionnaire

A total of 22 persons participated in the survey, 50% woman and 50% men with ages ranging from 20 to 50 years old. Those people were related to the IRTIC lab, as we wanted to have the feedback of people that had already interacted with ROMOT. We have asked them the following question for four different situations: "I would feel comfortable watching romantic/sex scenes in ROMOT in the following situations: (a) If I don't know the rest of the audience; (b) If I go with my fiancée/husband/wife, but we don't know the rest of the audience; (c) If I go with friends/colleagues; (d) If I go with my family/relatives (adults)". For each of the four situations and for each case study (romantic/sex) they had to give a score from 1 (completely disagree) to 5 (completely agree).

The results of the given answers are depicted in Fig. 10 (romantic case study) and Fig. 11 (sex case study). As it can be seen, when comparing the results of the different case studies, we can say that people would feel more comfortable having romantic experiences in ROMOT. When looking to the different situations for both scenarios, most people would feel uncomfortable when going with their family or relatives, especially in the sex case scenario. This happens even if the selected scene does not involve explicit sex content. However, most people would feel comfortable with the sex case scenario if they go with friends or colleagues.

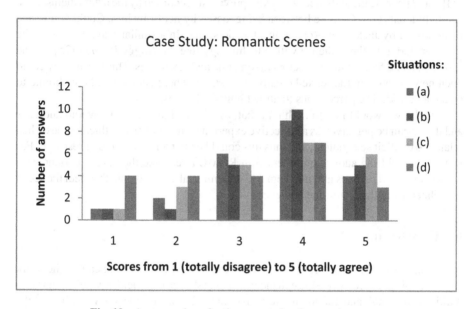

Fig. 10. Answers given for the case study of romantic scenes.

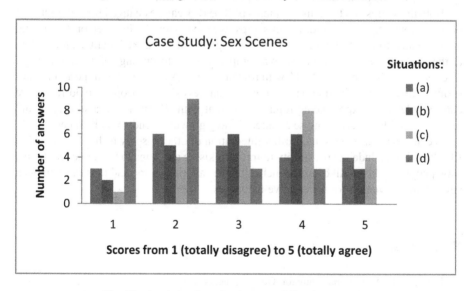

Fig. 11. Answers given for the case study of sex scenes.

5.3   Integrating Other Display Technologies

Also, other kind of display technologies could be included in ROMOT to enhance movies with other stimuli such as taste or touch. For instance, the *Kissinger* technology [24] could provide the audience with a kiss previously recorded by the actors themselves, and individuals could choose between being kissed by her or by him. Could you image being kissed by Jack or by Rose in the Titanic scene? In a similar way, hugs could be also transferred to the audience with a technology like the *Huggy Pajama* [25], so the audience could feel the hugs of actors in romantic and sex scenes. This technology could open new avenues in the related creative industries, where actors could collaborate to create a new kind of perceptions to attract huge audiences.

Finally, we would like to highlight that, as ROMOT involves the whole audience and thus it can be perceived as a collective experience, it could bring ethical issues when related to explicit sex content, and thus this could be an interesting field of research. For instance, would the audience immersed in ROMOT feel like they are experiencing a kind-of orgy and perhaps making them feel uncomfortable? Or would they feel the scene as isolated from the rest of the audience?

6   Conclusion

In this paper we have presented ROMOT, a robotized 3D-movie theatre. The work shown in this paper relates to the enhancement of audience experiences when integrating multimodal stimuli and making it interactive. In addition, we show the versatility of the system by means of the different kind of generated content.

Both the setups and the filmic contents of ROMOT can be changed for different kind of user experiences. As the different setups, we have shown a first-person movie and others related to the technologies of virtual, augmented and mixed realities. Regarding to the content, we have briefly shown samples related to driving safety and added a discussion for the use of ROMOT with romantic and sex content. To support our statements, a first user evaluation has been given that reveals that people would feel more comfortable when experiencing romantic content with ROMOT, but also they would feel comfortable experiencing sex content if they go with friends or colleagues.

We also have discussed the further integration of other display technologies within ROMOT that include the possibility to transmit kisses and hugs to the audience. In this way, people could feel like being touched by the favorite actors, and thus this can open new business avenues for the creative industries.

References

1. Heilig, M.L.: Sensorama simulator. Google Patents (1962)
2. Heilig, M.L.: El cine del futuro: the cinema of the future. Presence Teleoper. Virtual Environ. **1**, 279–294 (1992)

3. Robinett, W.: Interactivity and individual viewpoint in shared virtual worlds: the big screen vs. networked personal displays. SIGGRAPH. Comput. Graph. **28**, 127–130 (1994)
4. Ikei, Y., Okuya, Y., Shimabukuro, S., Abe, K., Amemiya, T., Hirota, K.: To relive a valuable experience of the world at the digital museum. In: Yamamoto, S. (ed.) HCI 2014. LNCS, vol. 8522, pp. 501–510. Springer, Cham (2014). doi:10.1007/978-3-319-07863-2_48
5. Matsukura, H., Yoneda, T., Ishida, H.: Smelling screen: development and evaluation of an olfactory display system for presenting a virtual odor source. IEEE Trans. Visual Comput. Graphics **19**, 606–615 (2013)
6. 4DX. http://www.cj4dx.com/about/about.asp
7. Pix 5D Cinema. http://expressavenue.in/?q=store/pix-5d-cinema
8. 5D cinema extreme. http://www.5dcinema.hu/
9. Yecies, B.: Transnational collaboration of the multisensory kind: exploiting Korean 4D cinema in China. Media Int. Australia **159**, 22–31 (2016)
10. Tryon, C.: Reboot cinema. Convergence: Int. J. Res. New Media Technol. **19**, 432–437 (2013)
11. http://www.xd-cinema.com/the-difference-between-4d-5d-6d-7d-8d-9d-xd-cinema/
12. Groen, E.L., Bles, W.: How to use body tilt for the simulation of linear self motion. J. Vestib. Res. **14**, 375–385 (2004)
13. Stewart, D.: A platform with six degrees of freedom (1965)
14. Casas, S., Coma, I., Riera, J.V., Fernández, M.: Motion-cuing algorithms: characterization of users' perception. Hum. Factors: J. Hum. Factors Ergon. Soc. **57**, 144–162 (2015)
15. Nahon, M.A., Reid, L.D.: Simulator motion-drive algorithms - a designer's perspective. J. Guid. Control Dyn. **13**, 356–362 (1990)
16. Casas, S., Coma, I., Portalés, C., Fernández, M.: Towards a simulation-based tuning of motion cueing algorithms. Simul. Model. Pract. Theory **67**, 137–154 (2016)
17. Küçük, S.: Serial and Parallel Robot Manipulators - Kinematics, Dynamics, Control and Optimization. InTech (2012)
18. Sinacori, J.B.: The Determination of Some Requirements for a Helicopter Flight Research Simulation Facility. Moffet Field (1977)
19. Olorama Technology. http://www.olorama.com/en/
20. Enttec. http://www.enttec.com/
21. Portalés, C., Gimeno, J., Casas, S., Olanda, R., Giner, F.: Interacting with augmented reality mirrors. In: Rodrigues, J., Cardoso, P., Monteiro, J., Figueiredo, M. (eds.) Handbook of Research on Human-Computer Interfaces, Developments and Applications, pp. 216–244. IGI-Global (2016)
22. IMSDb. http://www.imsdb.com/scripts/Titanic.html
23. Hypable. http://www.hypable.com/detailed-description-of-breaking-dawn-honeymoon-scene
24. Lovotics. http://kissenger.lovotics.com/
25. Teh, J.K.S., Cheok, A.D., Peiris, R.L., Choi, Y., Thuong, V., Lai, S.: Huggy Pajama: a mobile parent and child hugging communication system. In: Proceedings of the 7th International Conference on Interaction Design and Children, Chicago, Illinois, USA, 11–13 June 2008, Proceedings, pp. 250–257. ACM (2008)

For the Love of Artifice 2: Attachment

An Extension of the Paper 'for the Love of Artifice: Why We Need Robot Sex Dolls and Why There Is a Growing Sub Culture of Real People Trying to Become Them'

Trudy Barber[✉]

Faculty of Creative and Cultural Industries, School of Media and Performing Arts,
University of Portsmouth, Portsmouth, PO1 2DJ, UK
Trudy.Barber@port.ac.uk

Abstract. This work is an extension to the original paper written for the AISB 50 Conference Symposium by the author 'For the Love of Artifice: why we need robot sex dolls and why there is a growing subculture of people trying to become them' where 'evolutionary sexual strategies according to Buss and Schmidt were introduced as a lens for discussing relations with artificial humans. In addition, this paper has combined Money's discussion of love mapping with Schwartz and White's theoretical approaches to attachment as a framework to explore our individual sexual strategies with artificial partners. It is argued in this extended paper that such theoretical approaches should be combined to facilitate discourse on the impact of robotic and technological intimacy on the end user. This need not necessarily be solely seen in terms of psychological aspects, but also in relation to Jenkins' notion of contemporary participatory culture, associations with multi-mediated geek fandoms and fetishes, and concepts of social acceptance. As a consequence of this, elements of attachment explored as a sexual project rather than an emotional one, as in erotic countertransference onto robots and technology for example, will be developed.

Keywords: Attachment · Cybersex · Intimacy · Geeks · Fetish · Love maps · Nerds · Sex robots · Sexual strategies · Technology

1 Introduction

According to Ferguson [1], the contemporary sex doll or "fully functioning feminized android [...] appears to have arrived at the threshold of the boundary between pleasure and science."[1] As a consequence then, this paper will not re-visit popular associated discussions of misogyny, surrealist representations of the female form,[2] nor the female robot through science fiction and fantasy narrative [2] – but will explore in a similar

---

[1] Ferguson (2010, p. 3).
[2] Bellmer 1902–1975. For a general overview of his work see: https://en.wikipedia.org/wiki/Hans_Bellmer.

© Springer International Publishing AG 2017
A.D. Cheok et al. (Eds.): LSR 2016, LNAI 10237, pp. 64–71, 2017.
DOI: 10.1007/978-3-319-57738-8_6

fashion as to what has been argued [3] as the "spectre of necrophilia, [a] lens through which the sexualisation of artificial humans has been viewed."[3] In this light, this paper wishes to contrast the notion of making the artificial human as a sex toy - and it's associations with a deconstruction of what this paper terms the *datafication* of pleasure and, in this instance, the *geekification* of the end user - with what could be described by Buss and Schmidt [4] as the 'lens'of an evolutionary 'Sexual Strategies Theory', combined with the construction of a psychological 'Love Map' as argued by Money [5] together with 'Attachment Theory' as contextualized by Schwarz and White [6]. This combination will be used as a framework for exploring the construction of, and sexual engagement with, artifice.

2 Contemporary Context

For some, the idea of solitary engagement with high-tech artifice consolidates elements of intimate relations and possible emotional ties. Khan et al. [7] explain "that to understand deep parts of human-robot interaction – and of what it means to be a human – we need to assess the possibilities and limits of psychological intimacy with robots."[4] This in-turn reveals the potential capabilities of depth (or lack of it) of human to human intimacy. As suggested in the previous version of this paper - if this can be explored in terms of love and sex, we could also use artificial humans to understand sadism, cruelty, fear and violence. In which case would creating the features of hatred, anger, and sexual sadism for example be further challenging in the context of lengthy discussions surrounding the Uncanny Valley [8]? Hanson has argued that the "identification of fundamental principles of robot aesthetics can greatly accelerate the successful deployment of robots" [9]. So there needs to be specific fundamental principles that would be needed to develop sexual interaction and engagement in which contemporary robots would be categorised – similar to other forms of entertainment such as movie or TV genres. The artificial robot created for sexual entertainment then, through a process of datafication of its various programmable responses and behaviors, can be branded and launched as a consumer product aimed at specific sections of market preference. The robot doesn't just need to overcome our reactions to the Uncanny Valley, but also needs to satisfy a more sophisticated and, according to Jenkins, a transmediated[5] contemporary clientele who are used to having their specific inclinations and predilections catered for through narrative world-building and audience participation as enthusiasts and through fandom activities [10].

---

[3] de Fren (2009, p. 409).

[4] Khan et al. (2010, p. 124).

[5] For a definition and further discussion on transmedia see: http://henryjenkins.org/2011/08/defining_transmedia_further_re.html.

2.1 Popular Culture

The popularity of engagement with technological artifice such as robots ad sex dolls was discussed in the earlier version of this paper. To re-cap, it was argued that in contemporary narcissistic behaviors online (such as the 'selfie' for example) the concept of artifice, the robot and sex doll take on sexual and sub-cultural significance. This can be seen as evidence of forms of psychological transference which will be discussed in more detail in Sect. 3. Whereas gender identity has been argued extensively by Butler as something that is performative [11], there are other performed identities that include notions of the robot and sex doll which are freely exposed on the Internet. This is a sub-cultural fan base of androidism: those who wish to perform as and appear to be robots and dolls. Venus Angelic from the UK is one such participant with an extensive trans-media presence – Venus Youtube Videos explain how to get the 'android look'[6]. Using a technique redolent of the popular BBC 3 TV youth programming reality TV 'make-under show' *Snog Marry Avoid*[7], ironically Venus - in the 'step by step' video - demonstrates her 'make-over' transformation into an android doll. The video states 'for the ANDROID look you only need to wear ONE scleral lens.' The process demonstrated is hypnotic, invasive and appears to feed back into notions of the Uncanny Valley once more. So popular culture then, has a particular role to play when we consider our interaction with the idea of the sex doll/robot. This is just one simple example of how our experiences of the robot in popular culture can color responses and attitudes. This when combined with a sexual strategy theory create an explosive mix which could influence and affect the design and creation of artifice for pleasure. There are responses of revulsion, humor, inquisitiveness and even disbelief that such desires exist for sexual interaction with the artificial human or robot. However, it has also been contested that robots for sexual intimacy need not necessarily take on human form or likeness,[8] which could enable an even more innovative approach to creating inventions of pleasure. It is therefore argued that such creative approaches to pleasure are intrinsic to human nature, and should be included in articulations of 'evolutionary sexual strategy theory'.

3 Evolutionary Sexual Strategy

'A key ingredient of Sexual Strategies Theory is that mating strategies are context dependant, and in particular highly sensitive to the temporal context of short-term versus long-term mateships.'[9] In this quotation, Buss and Schmidt begin to lay out their Sexual Strategies Theory [4]. Should this viewpoint be applied to a sexual strategy of 'mateship' with artificial humans, the appreciation between long term commitments, versus short-term sexual release is revealed. This appreciation can vary from the type of investment

---

[6] Venus Angelic: How to look like an android doll http://www.youtube.com/watch?v=NU5NzchNkng.

[7] Snog Marry Avoid (2008-) BBC 3. Remarkable Television. UK.

[8] Devlin (2016), Keynote Address. Second International Congress on Love and Sex with Robots. Goldsmiths University. London. UK. http://loveandsexwithrobots.org/.

[9] Buss and Schmidt (1993, p. 205).

made for the specificities of artificial interaction – both emotionally and financially; and also reveals the context dependant on such participation with artificial humans. Buss and Schmitt postulate that 'long term mating, like all sexual strategies, carries costs when contrasted with alternative strategies.' [10] Evolutionary psychologists such as Buller [12] contest elements of such discussion and tend to argue around notions of *homogamy* and *assortative mating* mainly from a heterosexual standpoint and suggest that 'people tend to mate with those similar in race or ethnic background, age, socioeconomic status, educational background, and religious orientation.' [11] If this is applied to our relationship with technology and artificial humans and robots then, this also reveals something further about how our perceptions of intimacy have developed over chronological time and technological design time.

There are some interesting metaphorically descriptive discussions surrounding our psychology and subsequent interactions with technology and robots. The reliance of the socially interactive robot as being founded on deception has been considered as over-simplified by de Graaf [13]. However, in the past there have also been psychological descriptions of the human individual as a robot which is thought to be exhibited as part of narcissistic disorder and a representation of a 'pseudo-ego' [14]. There are also definitions of an automaton self and an automaton state in which an individual self-harms because of a lack of mutual reciprocity from others [15]. Inherent dangers of what is perceived as the unidirectional bond of the human with the robot have also been explored [16]. Much of these associations are seen as part of the general discourse of psychological disorders with possible social stigma and fear attached. It is therefore of no surprise that there appears to be a counter transference of such fears and stigma from society onto those who would have intimacy with robots and other technologies. On a personal level, the individual who may well engage in some form of transference with their chosen technology of pleasure are also engaging and investing in their own sexual strategy. In an empirical study by Scheutz and Arnold [17] it was argued that there is tension between technology and society when it comes to robot sex. They state:

> "The tension in technology between social distancing and achieved intimacy requires closer empirical study into exactly what conditions and contexts make autonomous systems more harmful than helpful. This is especially important for the design and use of robots in sexual contexts, given the intricate and powerful norms, expectations, and associations that sex carries with it." [12]

Our understanding of a socially embedded technological otherness is now articulated as part of our very sense of self and how we engage with our intimately and selectively mediated construction of identity needs further exploration. Part of that construction and exploration, and our sense of attachment both sexual and romantic, it is argued, also involves the process of love mapping. This would also apply to building our relationship with technology and interaction with robots.

---

[10] Buss and Schmidt (1993, p. 216).

[11] Buller (2005, p. 213).

[12] Scheutz and Arnold (2016, p. 358).

4   Love Mapping

According to Money [5] a "Lovemap"; is sexologically described as "a developmental representation or template of the mind and in the brain depicting the idealized lover and idealized program of sexuoerotic activity projected in imagery or actually engaged in with that lover."[13] It is argued that this constant search for the creation of an individual lovemap is how and why contemporary and emerging digital media are used, as love-mapping provides a tool with which to sublimate many forms of deviant, experimental or usual sexual practices, relationship tinkering, or to explore identity formation and gender.

In light of our current relationships to the artificial, it would appear that connections and attachments to technology is an amplification of a long standing and traditional argument surrounding deviancy that Money has discussed in detail. Downing [18] reviews this and suggests that Money, through his hypothetical constructionist theory surrounding lovemaps and the genesis of paraphilias, argues that this is evidence of "social developments that have gone awry", which it is argued, is different from more traditional "nineteenth-century understanding of *nature* gone awry."[14] It can therefore be suggested that the argument against the love of robots and our attachment to tech-nology in general can be compounded by the concept of 'nature' against 'social devel-opments' that deviate from tradition or what is considered a 'normative' understanding of human relationships – which in itself is contested. Lovemapping has been discussed by sexologists Benestad, Almå and Weingarten as the creation of "turn-on patterns."[15] They have discovered that through the exploration of lovemapping individuals have been able to identify and enjoy their turn-on patterns and find positive and ethical ways of practicing them [19]. This sex-positive approach would better contextualize the concept of lovemapping that includes relationships with robots. An example of this would be the engagement of a woman to her robot in hopes of marriage in the future. Not only does this challenge notions of human to robot relationships but also ethical issues, as well as the enactment of a more traditional lovemap involving heterosexual commitment.[16]

So the concept of 'lovemapping' in this context of humans doing so with robots, can be argued in terms of a manifestation of deviated social development, which this paper argues, can lead to even more original approaches to innovation and technological development. In our 'desire to be wired' there is also a revelation that openly displays our need to be connected. The examples in this paper explain how deviant sexual practices instigated by our push to find our individual sexual strategy and our love map extend the boundaries of technological development and emerging media and ethical engagement. However, it is not solely the technological hardware that needs to be developed it is also the content of such mediated behavior that inspires attachment that needs to be considered.

---

[13] Money (1986, p. 290).

[14] Downing (2010, pp. 277–278).

[15] Benestad et al. (2015, p. 27).

[16] See: http://futureofsex.net/robots/lilly-inmoovator-engaged-human-robot-couple-want-right-marry/.

5   Attachment

Schwarz and White [6] argue that "attachment is seen as a source of human motivation as fundamental as those of food and sex."[17] They go on to contest Bowlby's [20] postulation "that attachment behavior is any form of behavior that results in a person attaining or maintaining proximity to some other preferred and differentiated individual."[18] They suggest that "sexuality was not a focus of theoretical concern for Bowlby" and that "he emphasized that attachment was a motivational system in its own right, apart from sexuality and feeding" (see Footnote 17). Like other relational theories, Schwarz and White argue that attachment theory has been criticized for its failure to theorize sexuality adequately in light that "it has come to be understood that attachment is a bodily experience"[19]. They cite Mitchell [21] as evidence here, and argue that "within contemporary relational theories, sexuality has come to be seen as the central arena in which the dramas of attachment are played out— in which "emotional connection and intimacy is sought, established, lost and regained"[20] (see Footnote 17). It is also suggested therefore, that intimacy and attachment to a robot or technological other for example, adds a new dimension to what had been discussed and theorized as 'adult attachment styles' by Hudson-Allez [22]. Such articulations should be considered as value potential for integrative theoretical models for advancing relationship science, as well as providing insight into attachment related behaviors such "as safe-haven and secure-based functions",[21] similar to those of a human attachment figure [23].

Dewitte's [24] review on sex, attachment and human to human relationships, argues that it is important to focus on "the processes that mediate the link between sex and attachment"[22]. Dewitte confirms that part of the process of focus within this research is to explore an emotion–motivational model in combination with evolutionary and attachment perspectives. She states that "the emotion–motivational perspective specifies the different processes and pathways through which attachment schemas influence sexual responses."[23] By conceptualizing the attachment and the sexual system in terms of emotion regulation Dewitte suggests would set up new and alternative lines of inquiry into sex and attachment. If this approach to research is translated directly to sexual activity between humans, sex robots and artificial humans, it may prove invaluable as to how to explore the process of attachment that we generate with our technologies of pleasure. This may also be able to explain whether we feel that there are potential processes that could also be translated from a transverse viewpoint; that of whether robots can become attached to humans. Robots could then not only feel attachment to humans, but would also have the potential to be attached to each other.

---

[17] Schwarz and White (2005, p. 7).
[18] Bowlby (1979, p. 129).
[19] Ibid.
[20] Mitchell (1988, p. 107).
[21] Birnbaum et al. (2016, p. 417).
[22] Dewitte (2012, p. 119).
[23] Dewitte (2012, p. 120).

6 Summary

This paper has brought together approaches from different disciplines in order to engage with concepts of robot sex. It has argued that through the use of robots, stimulation and communication technology or artificial humans for sexual interaction, an individual can test out their own issues surrounding attachment and intimacy. This is inclusive of the continuous recreation, re-affirmation and performance or 'acting out' of a psychological love map that induces attachment to the object or device concerned as part of an individual and personalized sexual strategy. However, due to various portrayals of robots in popular culture, sex with robots can be seen as a manifestation of a deviant form of social development that some may find awkward and associated with counter transference and stigma. This is all too easily associated with another conceptual context articulating that such behavior is 'against nature' and part of the Frankenstein approach to technology, in that it has the potential to be 'out of control' and therefore dangerous. There is a feminist movement – The Campaign Against Sex Robots – that aims to ban sex and technological activities along with anthropomorphic and animistic articulations which are redolent of radical Dworkinite fears and the demeaning of sex workers in general and women in particular. However, it is argued that this can also be seen a contemporary example of deviation as key to innovation [25] and as a blatant opportunity to explore sexuality and the human condition in even more depth in a sex-positive way that reveals more about our need to be creative, innovative and inventive as part of our human evolutionary sexual strategy as a whole. In conclusion, it is hoped that the development of robots and artificial humans that may be able to respond to us and to each other will contribute to the evolution of our sense of sexual self and may eventually break the notion of a feared unidirectional approach to relationships, to emerging technologies and eventually, to love.

References

1. Ferguson, A.: The Sex Doll: A History. McFarland Publishing, London (2010)
2. Barber, T.: Kinky Borgs and sexy robots: the fetish, fashion and discipline of seven of nine. In: Geraghty, L. (ed.) Future Visions: Key Science Fiction and Fantasy Television Texts, pp. 133–148. Scarecrow Press, Lanham (2009)
3. de Fren, A.: Technofetishism and the Uncanny Desires of A.S.F.R. (alt.sex.fetish.robots). Sci. Fict. Stud. **36**(3), 404–440 (2009). SF-TH Inc.
4. Buss, D., Schmitt, D.: Sexual strategies theory: an evolutionary perspective on human mating. Psychol. Rev. **100**(2), 204–232 (1993)
5. Money, J.: Lovemaps: Clinical Concepts of Sexual/Erotic Health and Pathology, Paraphilia and Gender Transposition in Childhood, Adolescence and Maturity. Irvington, New York (1986)
6. Schwartz, J., White, K. (eds.): Sexuality and Attachment in Clinical Practice. Karnac Books, London (2005)
7. Kahn, Jr. P.H., Ruckert, J.H., Kanda, T., Ishiguro, H., Reichert, A., Gary, H., Shen, S.: Psychological intimacy with robots? Using interaction patterns to uncover depth of relation. In: Proceedings of the 5th ICM/IEEE International Conference on Human – Robot Interaction (2010)

8. Mori, M.: The uncanny valley. Energy **7**(4), 33–35 (1970)

9. Hanson, D.: Exploring the aesthetic range for humanoid robots. In: Proceedings of the ICCS/CogSci-2006 Symposium: Toward Social Mechanisms of Android Science, Vancouver, Canada (2006)

10. Jenkins, H.: Convergence Culture: Where Old and New Media Collide. New York University Press, New York (2006)

11. Butler, J.: Gender Trouble: Feminism and the Subversion of Identity. Routledge, London (1990)

12. Buller, D.J.: Adapting Minds: Evolutionary Psychology and the Persistent Quest for Human Nature. MIT Press, Cambridge (2005)

13. de Graaf, M.M.A.: An ethical evaluation of human-robot relationships international. J. Soc. Robot. **8**(4), 589–598 (2016)

14. Ledermann, R.: The robot personality in narcissistic disorder. J. Anal. Psychol. **26**, 329–344 (1981)

15. Sweet, A.D.: The automaton self: defensive organisation, psychodynamics and treatment approaches. Psychodyn. Pract. **17**(4), 387–402 (2011)

16. Scheutz, M.: The inherent dangers of unidirectional emotional bonds between humans and socially interactive robots. In: Lin, P., Abney, K., Bekey, G.A. (eds.) Robot Ethics: The Ethical and Social Implications of Robotics. MIT Press, Cambridge (2012)

17. Scheutz, M., Arnold, T.: Are we ready for sex robots? In: 11th ACM/IEEE International Conference on Human Robot Interaction (HRI) (2016)

18. Downing, L.: John Money's 'Normophilia': diagnosing sexual normality in late-twentieth-century Anglo-American sexology. Psychol. Sex. **1**(3), 275–287 (2010)

19. Benestad, E.E.P., Almå, E., Weingarten, K.: Sex-positive ways of perceiving sex turn-on patterns. Part 1: understanding. Int. J. Narrative Ther. Community Work (1), 26–45 (2015)

20. Bowlby, J.: The Making and Breaking of Affectional Bonds. Tavistock, London (1979)

21. Mitchell, S.A.: Sex without drive (theory). In: Mitchell, S.A. (ed.) Relational Concepts in Psychoanalysis. Harvard University Press, Cambridge (1988)

22. Hudson-Allez, G.: Infant Losses; Adult Searches: A Neural and Developmental Perspective on Psychopathology and Sexual Offending. Karnac Books, London (2010)

23. Birnbaum, G.E., Mizrahi, M., Hoffman, G., Reis, H.T., Finkel, E.J., Sass, O.: What Robots can teach us about intimacy: The reassuring effects of robot responsiveness to human disclosure. Comput. Hum. Behav. **63**, 416–423 (2016)

24. Dewitte, M.: Different perspectives on the sex-attachment link: towards an emotion-motivational account. J. Sex Res. **49**(2–3), 105–124 (2012)

25. Barber, T.: Deviation as key to innovation: understanding a culture of the future. Foresight **6**(3), 141–152 (2004)

Influences on the Intention to Buy a Sex Robot

An Empirical Study on Influences of Personality Traits and Personal Characteristics on the Intention to Buy a Sex Robot

Jessica M. Szczuka[✉] and Nicole C. Krämer

Social Psychology: Media and Communication, University Duisburg-Essen,
Duisburg, Germany
{jessica.szczuka,nicole.kraemer}@uni-due.de

Abstract. The first sex robots will hit the market within the next few years, but no empirical research has gathered insights into the question who possible costumers could be. Therefore, the present study aimed to investigate personal characteristics (e.g. relationship status) and personality traits (such as loneliness) that would influence the intention to buy a Sex Robot. An online survey with 263 male participants showed that 40.3% would buy such a robot now or within the next five years. We could show that while the affiliation-related personality traits, the relationship status and sexual fulfilment does not have any impact on the intention to buy a sex robot, rather, negative attitude towards robots and anthropomorphic tendency are influential.

Keywords: Sex robots · Intention to buy · Personal characteristics

1 Introduction

With the rise of humanoid robots, more and more companies focus on building android robots (robotic replications of humans). As every human experiences sexual tensions, it seems plausible that those robots will also be built to satisfy sexual needs. Since the adult industry is known for driving technological developments, such as Internet applications or virtual reality [1], it can be expected that using robots for the satisfaction of sexual needs will soon be rendered possible due to the technological progress in the field of sex robots. Sex dolls increasingly have a hyper realistic outer appearance [2]. Companies, such as Abyss Creations, already work on different robotic solutions in order to enable the human replications to move and talk. The hyper realistic dolls cost about 6000 dollars each and the company makes about two million dollars per year, which underlines how profitable the market sector already is. The robotic versions will not only be more valuable because they are composed of cutting-edge technological components, but also because they will offer more social features (e.g. moving and talking). David Levy, one of the first researchers who discussed love and sex with robots in detail, predicted that by the year of 2050, robots will be capable of being "perceived as being similar to biological creatures" [3] (p. 303) and that this will make robots appealing in terms of sexual and affectional purposes. Despite these prospects, empirical research in

© Springer International Publishing AG 2017
A.D. Cheok et al. (Eds.): LSR 2016, LNAI 10237, pp. 72–83, 2017.
DOI: 10.1007/978-3-319-57738-8_7

the field of sexual aspects of human-robot interaction is almost non-existent. A first study with a relatively small male sample size by Schuetz and Arnold revealed that more than two thirds of the male participants could imagine to use a sex robot [4] which gives a first empirical evidence that the topic, as futuristic as it might seem, could be of interest for more than only a fringe group. Besides that, no empirical research gathered insights about who potential costumers could be. However, the media (press and films) often associates the usage of sex dolls or sex robots with being lonely (e.g. "Lonely men to get guide on building a sex robot" [5]) or having social anxieties (e.g. "Lars and the girl"). And indeed, it seems imaginable that people who suffer from social deficits might use controllable technology to satisfy sexual and affiliation-related needs, which all humans have.

In line with this, the goal of the present study was not only to investigate whether men could imagine to buy such a sex robot now of within the next five years, but more precisely which personality traits (e.g. loneliness or need to belong) and which personal characteristics (relationship status and perceived sexual fulfillment) as well as previous attitudes towards robots and technology in general (anthropomorphism and attitude towards robots) influence this decision.

It needs be noted that the presented data are part of a larger study which is submitted elsewhere (Szczuka & Krämer, revise and resubmit [6]). The other paper, however, does not include the main dependent variable of interest under consideration here, intention to buy. In contrast to the present study, also pictures of real women in underwear were shown.

2 Theory

2.1 Sex Robots

Sex robots can be understood as android robots (robotic replications of the appearances of women or men) that are built to satisfy sexual needs. For this purpose, the robots do not only provide replications of some secondary sexual characteristics (e.g. breasts), but also external genitals (e.g. labia). As this description would also be suitable for hyper realistic sex dolls, sex robots are also capable to move (especially with respect to movement which is important with regard to the fulfilment of sexual needs) and speak. Affective computing will be an important aspect of sex robots, since having sex is one of the most intimate interactions, in which reacting and acting like a human will be perceived as quality attribute. At present, there is no sex robot available that is suitable for masses and that provides all the features listed above. However, there are first approaches, such as the first moving body parts created by the company Abyss Creations. David Levy predicts that, by 2050, technological achievements will make it possible to fall in love, have sex and even get married with a robot [3]. On the other hand, there are, as mentioned above, ethical concerns raised with regard to those new developments. Among other aspects, the possible process of objectification (especially with respect to prostitutes) needs to be kept in mind, as well as the illusion of love (caused by the illusion of interaction with a person) that can lead to various ramifications [7, 8].

Research on sex robots is nearly non-existent and therefore no research has focused on the possible consumer so far. As mentioned in the introduction, so far there are no Sex Robots on the market which would allow an investigation of real interactions between humans and Sex Robots. Therefore, the current research needs to rely on more indirect concepts, such as the purchase intention. Purchase intention is defined as "individual's readiness and willingness to purchase a certain product or service' [9] and implies a positive evaluation. As we are used to the process of purchasing products, this variable enables participants to estimate the consequences (e.g. paying for the article, using it). Concerning the purchase of sex toys, sex dolls (ranging from cheap inflatable versions to expensive ones made of silicone) and technology that is used for sexual stimulation are already part of the present sex toy industry [10]. Reece et al. asked 1047 males about their experiences with vibrators and the results showed that 45% of the sample indicated to incorporate vibrators into sexual activities and it needs to be highlighted that buying products to enhance the sexual life has become more and more socially accepted due to better products, more ways to purchase those products (e.g. online) and cultural changes (e.g. the publication of E.L. James' "Fifty Shades of Grey" caused a growth of the market) [11]. Even though some of the products are built to stimulate one person at a time, research on the acceptance of vibrators showed that women accepted the usage of this technology as a part of a healthy relationship [12]. Based on the fact that no empirical data could be found with regard to men and their usage of sex toys in relationships and the influence of sexual fulfilment the following research questions are asked:

RQ1: Is there a difference between singles and males in relationships with regard to the intention to buy a sex robot?

RQ2: Is there a difference between males who rate their sex life to be fulfilling and those who rate their sex life to be unfulfilled with regard to the intention to buy a sex robot?

2.2 Influence of Sexual and Social Norms

The intention to buy a sex robot may be influenced by sexual and social norms. Nowadays, technology plays an important role in sexuality [10–13] and there is even a name for it: The term technosexuality describes sexual activities that are combined with technology. There are technosexual behaviors, such as internet pornography, that are more common than others. So far, sexual activities involving robots have been described as deviant and termed as robot fetishism. It is defined as "fetish attraction to humanoid or non-humanoid robots, or to people behaving like robots, or to people dressed in robot costumes" [10] (pp. 66, 67). Even though possible users might not be aware of the fact that such a sexual behavior could be labeled as fetishism, it is obvious that sexual activities with an object is deviant of statistical sexual norms [2], which in turn could be evaluated negatively. Moreover, these sexual norms could lead to difficulties in the context of empirical research, as participants have the tendency to respond in ways that they believe to be socially accepted (social desirability).

Another aspect that could lead to negative attitudes towards sex robots is that having sex with a doll, instead of a human, is associated with being lonely or desperate [10].

Even though a robot is more lifelike compared to a doll, it is still a machine and therefore it can be assumed that this stereotype could transfer to sex robots, as both are non-human.

2.3 Influence of Personal Characteristics in HRI

Affiliation-related variables in the context of (sex) robots.

Thinking about sex doll or future sex robot owners, there is a stereotype (often portrayed by the media, e.g. in the news such as Fullerton or in the film Lars and the Real Girl) claiming that people who are attracted by artificial entities suffer from loneliness or are not able to get in touch with other people [5, 14]. David Levy also addressed this topic in his book "Love and Sex with Robots" by stating in his conclusion "Many who would otherwise have become social misfits, social outcasts, or even worse will instead be better-balanced human beings." [3] (p. 304). A documentation named "Guys and Dolls" produced by Flintoff and Raphael portrayed owners of real dolls and one thirty-two-year-old man confirmed Levy's conclusion by saying: "I can tolerate being alone, but not loneliness" [2, 15]. Even though there are no empirical results with regard to sex robots, research could show that lonely people do benefit of contact with humanoid robots. For instance, Eyssel and Reich demonstrated that lonely people tend to anthropomorphize humanoid robots more strongly (with respect to their characteristics) [16]. This finding is of relevance, since people have a fundamental motivation to affiliate with others [17] which in turn could be satisfied by interactions with humanoid robots. It is therefore conceivable that especially people who have problems satisfying their need to belong, such as people with social anxieties, might benefit from interactions with humanoid robots. They could provide safety with respect to aspects or behaviors that could be controlled in a robot, such as fear of rejection [18]. This aspect might be of special importance for sex robots, since people suffering from social anxieties have problems to engage in interactions with the opposite sex and consequently they have less sexual experiences in their lives [19]. A first empirical hint in the direction how people suffering from social anxieties can benefit by interactions with robots was provided by Suzuki, Yamada, Kanda and Nomura who conducted a study in which they examined people who had higher scores for social avoidance and distress [20]. The results showed that they would prefer robots over humans as communication partners in various situations (e.g. asking directions at a station or on the street).

Pre-existing Attitudes

Another aspect that could be important with regard to the purchase intention of sex robots is that robots, as a concept, are associated with certain pre-existing positive and negative biases [21]. In this context, Nomura, Suzuki, Kanda and Kato investigated anxieties people have towards robots with regard to situations in which people have to interact with robots, towards the social influence of robots and towards emotions robots could have [22]. They developed the negative attitude towards robots scale (NARS), which is an important instrument in the research on human-robot-interaction. Different studies showed that the NARS has an influence on diverse evaluations in human-robot-interactions. For instance, the NARS has an influence on the distance people keep between robots and themselves and the willingness to engage in physical contact with robots [23]. Here, no research has been conducted so far that focusses on sex robots and pre-existing attitudes.

Based on the listed results the following hypothesis was derived:

H1: Loneliness, importance of social contacts, fear of rejection, the individual degree of interaction deficits, anthropomorphic tendency and the negative attitude towards robots are predictors of the intention to buy a sex robot now or within the next five years.

3   Method

3.1   Sample and Procedure

To investigate the explicit evaluation of sex robots, a total of 263 heterosexual male participants between the age of 18 to 67 (M = 25.89, SD = 6.80) took part in an online survey. Nine participants were excluded from the analysis. The decision of exclusion is statistically based on the analysis of the corresponding boxplot. (52.9%) (N = 139) of the participants indicated that they were in a relationship while 124 were single. With regard to their sexual life, 135 participants (51.3%) named that they had a fulfilling sexual life, while the other 128 males (48.7%) rated their own sexual life to be unfulfilling.

The present study focused on male participants only, which is based on three important aspects. (1) Attitudes related to sexual activities differ strongly in men and women, (2) an empirical study conducted by Schuetz and Arnold showed that men were significantly more in favor with sex robots, respectively the idea of using one, compared to women and (3) the product sector focusses more on the male consumer by producing mainly female sex dolls or (first) sex robots [4, 24].

The survey was composed of three parts. First, they had to watch a video of two minutes showing female robots, such as Sophia (by Hanson Robotics) and HRP-4C (Miim; by the National Institute of Advanced Industrial Science and Technology (AIST)). This was important in order to create a mutual understanding of what state-of-the-art robots do look like (e.g. facial expressions, secondary sexual characteristics), what their abilities are (e.g. standing and walking) and in which fields of application they can be used in (e.g. domestic worker or training object for dentists). The second block was composed of different personality measures which will be explained in more detail in the next section. In the last section the participates had to rate the attractiveness of four pictures of women in underwear, four pictures of female robots in underwear with salient mechanical body parts and four pictures of female androids (biologically correct replication of women) in underwear. There was a note under every picture clarifying whether the picture displayed a women or a robot. After that, the males were asked whether they would buy such a robot for themselves now or within the five next years and to indicate why and what they evaluated to be attractive and unattractive with regards to the female robots in underwear with salient mechanical body parts and the female androids (biologically correct replication of women) in underwear via text field. Finally, each participant received a debriefing and had the chance to win 3 × 50 € gift certificate.

3.2   Stimulus Material

In order to ensure comparableness of the pictures of the female robots in underwear with salient mechanical body parts and the female androids (biologically correct replication of women) in underwear it is important to mention that the displayed robots all wore black and white basic underwear, that they were all shown against a white background, that all the pictures showed the same image section and that they all had a neutral to sexy look on their faces. Moreover, the pictures were selected based on a pretest (N = 10) in order to exclude the pictures of robots who were rated unrealistic and particularly attractive/unattractive. Figure 1 shows examples of the stimulus material.

Fig. 1. Examples for the stimulus material of the robots without salient mechanical body parts (left) and the robots with salient mechanical body parts (right).

3.3   Measures

In the following, all dependent and independent variables are explained. Please note that all used scales had to be answered on a 5-point Likert scale (1 = "disagree strongly" to 5 = "agree strongly"). Moreover, there were two more used measurements (a self-provided scale measuring the concept of suspension of disbelief and a self-developed scale measuring the importance of the social aspects of sex) which could not be used in further analyses due to an unsatisfying level of internal consistency ($\alpha \geq 0.5$).

Anthropomorphic tendency.   To assess whether the participants have the "tendency to ascribe human characteristics to non-human objects" (p. 214) the Anthropomorphism Questionnaire by Neave, Jackson, Saxton, & Hönekopp was used [25]. Even though the scale was originally developed to measure the influence of anthropomorphic tendencies on hoarding, the 20 items, such as "Part of the reason why I picked a new car/electrical item was because when I first saw it I felt that it had a friendly personality" are worded neutrally and could therefore be used in the present study. The internal consistency was $\alpha = .891$.

Negative attitudes towards robots. The NARS scale by Syrdal, Dautenhahn, Koay and Walters covers negative attitudes towards situations and interactions with robots, social influence of robots and emotions in interactions with robots [21]. The 11 items (e.g. "I would feel uneasy if robots really had emotions") had an internal consistency (Cronbach's alpha) of $\alpha = .819$.

Loneliness. The revised UCLA Loneliness scale by Russel, Peplau and Cutrona was used to assess one's subjective feelings of loneliness [26]. The 20 items (e.g. "People are around me but not with me") had an internal consistency of $\alpha = .914$.

Need to belong (Importance of social contacts). The subscale "importance of social contacts" of the need to belong scale by Krämer et al. was used to measure the importance of the contact to others in the everyday life [27]. The subscale consists of five items (e.g. "I frequently think of my loved ones"). The internal consistency (Cronbach's alpha) was $\alpha = .772$.

Social anxiety (Fear of Rejection & Interaction deficit). The SASKO Scale of Social Anxiety by Kolbeck contains the subscales "fear of rejection" and "interaction deficit" [18]. Each subscale contains five items, such as "I am afraid of situations in which I could get rejected by somebody of the opposite gender." and "I feel uneasy at parties because I don't know how to behave". The subscales "fear of rejection" had a Cronbach's Alpha of $\alpha = .826$, while the other subscale "interaction deficit" reached an internal consistency of $\alpha = .746$.

4   Results

4.1   Differences with Regard to Relationship Status and Fulfillment of Sexual Life (RQ1 & RQ2)

Two Chi-square tests of independence were computed in order to see whether there would be differences between singles and males in relationships as well as between males that would rate their own sexual life as fulfilling and unfulfilling with regard to the question whether they could imagine to buy a sex robot now or within the next five years. No significant relation between relationship status and the question whether males would buy a sex robot ($\chi^2(1) = .248, p = .62$) could be found, nor was there a relation between the subjective rating of sexual fulfillment and the willingness to buy such a robot ($\chi^2(1) = .37, p = .54$).

4.2   Influence of Personality Traits on Intention to Buy (H1)

In general, it has to be noted that 40.3% of the present sample indicated that they could imagine to buy a sex robot now or within the next five years.

A logistic regression analysis was conducted to predict whether one could imagine buying such a robot now or within the next five years using anthropomorphic tendency, physical self-concept, negative attitudes towards robots, loneliness, importance of social contacts, fear of rejection and the individual degree of interaction deficits. A test of the full model against a constant only model was statistically significant, indicating that the predictors as a set reliably distinguished between men that would buy a sex robot now or within the next five years and men that would not buy such a robot $(\chi^2(6) = 58.74, p \leq .01, N = 263)$. Overall model fit was acceptable/good (Hosmer and Lemeshow $\chi^2(8) = 8.80, p = 0.36$; Nagelkerke's $R^2 = 0.27$) (Backhaus, Erichson, Plinke, & Weiber, 2000). Prediction success overall was 70.3% (79.6% for decline and 56.6% for accept). The Wald criterion however demonstrated that merely anthropomorphic tendency ($\beta = .777$, Wald $= 8.36$, p $= .00$, Exp(B) $= 2.18$, CI $= 1.29 - 3.68$) and egative attitude towards robots ($\beta = -1.60$, Wald $= 38.378, p \leq .01$, Exp(B) $= .20$, p $\leq .01$, CI $= .12 - .34$) made a significant contribution to prediction. Exp(B) value indicates that when the anthropomorphic tendency is raised by one unit (here 5-point-Likert scale) males are almost twice as much willing to buy a sex robot now or within the next five years, while increasing negative attitudes towards robots by one unit (also 5-point-Likert scale) reduces the likelihood of buying such a robot also almost twice as much. As all the affiliation-related personality traits (loneliness, need to belong, social anxiety) were none-significant, the hypothesis needs to be rejected.

5   Discussion

The present study aimed to find aspects that would influence the intention to buy a sex robot now or within the next five years. The results not only empirically underline that the phenomenon sex robot is not just of interest for a fringe group, but also that many of aspects that have been considered to play a role (for example loneliness or the relationship status) were not as important as assumed.

In general, it has to be noted that 40.3% of the present sample indicated that they could imagine to buy a sex robot now or within the next five years. This is fully in line with a study by Schuetz and Arnold who showed that more than two thirds of the males could imagine to use a sex robot [4]. This is an interesting result, as it was imaginable that males would not indicate this, based on social and sexual norms or social desirability in the context of the empirical study. This also highlights that sex robots could be of interest for more than only a fringe group.

5.1   Differences with Regard to Relationship Status and Fulfillment of Sexual Life (RQ1 & RQ2)

The data showed that the possible consumers' relationship status and sexual fulfilment makes no difference with regard to a purchase intention of a sex robot. This is somewhat surprising, because the data do not support the assumption that sex robots would only be interesting as a substitute for frequent and fulfilling sexual intercourse. With regard to the importance of the costumers' relationship status, more research needs to be conducted, in order to gather insights about whether men (and also females) in relationships perceive sexual intercourse with a human-like machine as a form of being unfaithful or not. Moreover, it would be interesting to see for what kind of sexual experiences robots will be used. With regard to men in relationships one possible usage could be threesome sexual activities, which could explain that there is no difference with regard to the intention to buy a sex robot of men in relationships compared to singles.

On the other hand, not all singles and people who do not rate their sex life to be unfulfilling might be attracted to the idea of having sex with a robot. All in all, this result shows that possible costumers of sex robots can hardly be categorized by simple socio-demographic variables.

5.2 Influence of Personality Traits on Intention to Buy (H1)

The results of the logistic regression analysis showed that only anthropomorphic tendency and negative attitude towards robots were significant predictors and that all the affectional-related personal characteristics (e.g. loneliness) had no influence on the influence to buy a sex robot. Given prior results, the influence of negative attitudes towards robots is highly plausible: Nomura et al. showed that the negative attitude towards robots has an important impact on the evaluations of situations in which robots and humans get closer, meaning that it influences the allowed distance between robots and humans and the willingness to engage in touch with robots [22]. And as those are aspects that play a huge role in the context of sexual interactions, the predictor is plausible.

On the other hand, anthropomorphic tendency was the other significant predictor for the intention to buy sex robots. First of all, this indicated that the easier people imagine "life" in an artificial entity, the more compelling they think an artificial sex partner to be. On the other hand, this result suggests that sex robots need to be highly anthropomorphic in order to be attractive for possible costumers. As sex is such an intimate interaction it can be assumed that the males do prefer familiar aspects in a sexual "partner". More research needs to be done as it is imaginable that users see more in sex robots as just machines. This result could be a first evidence for this assumption.

This both highlights the importance of human likeness in the context of sex robots.

Moreover, this result highlights that affectional related characteristics, meaning the perceived loneliness, the importance of social contacts, fear or rejection and interaction deficits were all no predictors for intention to buy sex robots. This result shows that the picture of a lonely user who is not capable to bond with real people and instead uses a sex doll or robot was not confirmed empirically [5, 28].

5.3 Limitation and Further Research

One limitation could be seen in the fact that the data is self-reported. As sex robots are a topic that is influenced by social and sexual norms, this could mean that participants did not indicate their sexual preferences and/or that they gave answers that would form a certain impression (e.g. upright or eager to try out new things). Another important limitation is that the participants were not aware of the costs of a sex robot.

Moreover, we recruited the participants via social networking sites and newspaper ads in which we stated that the study would be about the evaluation of robots and the sexual aspects of human-robot-interaction (which needed to be done in order to clarify that the study would assess intimate data). However, it is possible that in the sense of self-selection mainly men took part in the study who were already open minded towards the topic of sex robots.

From a more general perspective, we argue that there is a strong need for future research focusing on the user and his or her acceptance for sex robots. And it should be a long-term goal to investigate real interactions between humans and sex robots, as research in the context of the uncanny valley phenomenon could already show that results differ based on the form of the stimulus material [8]. Since sex robots are mainly built by the adult industry, researchers rely on their technological developments in order to improve the quality of research. However, first empirical approaches using different kinds of stimulus material, such as pictures, videos or virtual reality and different forms of qualitative or quantitative measures should be encouraged in order to get new insights into the users' acceptance of sex robots as well as – probably more importantly – their effects.

6 Conclusion

The present study focused on the question who possible sex robot costumers could be. The data demonstrated that the phenomenon of sex robots is of interest for not just a fringe group and that the relationship status and the perceived fulfilment of the sexual life is not as important as assumed. More importantly, the results of the present study did not confirm the stereotype of lonely costumers, who would buy a sex robot because they suffer from social deficits. Instead, the negative attitude towards robots and the anthropomorphic tendency seem to play an important role.

References

1. Barss, P.: The Erotic Engine: How Pornography has Powered Mass Communication, from Gutenberg to Google. Doubleday Canada, Toronto (2011)
2. Worthen, M.G.: Sexual Deviance and Society: A Sociological Examination. Routledge, Abingdon (2016)
3. Levy, D.: Love and sex with robots: The evolution of human-robot relationships. New York (2007)
4. Schuetz, M., Arnold, T.: Are we ready for sex robots? In: The Eleventh ACM/IEEE International Conference on Human Robot Interation, pp. 351–358. IEEE Press (2016)
5. Fullerton, J.: Lonely men to get guide on building a sex robot, The Times, Newspaper article (2016). http://www.thetimes.co.uk/article/lonely-men-to-get-guide-on-building-a-sex-robot-hn69zggs0
6. Szczuka, J.M., Krämer, N.C. (revise and resubmit): Not Only the Lonely. How males explicitly and implicitly evaluate the attractiveness of sex robots in comparison to women and personal characteristics that influence this evaluation. Special Issue: Love and Sex with Robots. Multimodal Technologies and Interaction (2017)

7. Richardson, K.: The asymmetrical 'relationship': parallels between prostitution and the development of sex robots. ACM SIGCAS Comput. Soc. **45**(3), 290–293 (2016)
8. Sullins, J.P.: Applied Professional Ethics for the Reluctant Roboticist. Portland, OR, US. The Emerging Policy and Ethics of Human-Robot Interaction workshop at HRI (2015)
9. Ajzen, I., Fishbein, M.: Understanding Attitudes and Predicting Social Behavior. Prentice Hall, Englewood Cliffs (1980)
10. Ferguson, A.: The Sex Doll: A History. Mcfarland & Co Inc., USA (2010)
11. Reece, M., Herbenick, D., Dodge, B., Sanders, S.A., Ghassemi, A., Fortenberry, J.D.: Vibrator use among heterosexual men varies by partnership status: results from a nationally representative study in the United States. J. Sex Marital Ther. **36**(5), 389–407 (2010)
12. Herbenick, D., Reece, M., Schick, V., Jozkowski, K.N., Middelstadt, S.E., Sanders, S.A., Dodge, B.S., Ghassemi, A., Fortenberry, J.D.: Beliefs about women's vibrator use: results from a nationally representative survey in the United States. J. Sex Marital Ther. **37**(5), 329–345 (2011)
13. Bardzell, S., Bardzell, J.: Technosexuality. In: Wong, A., Wickramasinghe, M., Hoogland, R., Naples, N.A. (eds.) The Wiley Blackwell Encyclopedia of Gender and Sexuality Studies, pp. 1–3. John Wiley & Sons, Ltd., Singapore (2016)
14. Gillespie, C.: Lars and the Real Girl, USA (2007)
15. Flintoff, T., Raphael, M.: Guys and dolls [Motion picture documentary]. [Directed by N. Holt]. [Narrated by M. Strong]. North One-BBC America, United Kingdom (2006)
16. Eyssel, F., Reich, N.: Loneliness makes the heart grow fonder (of robots): on the effects of loneliness on psychological anthropomorphism. In: Proceedings of the 8th ACM/IEEE International Conference on Human-Robot Interaction, pp. 121–122. IEEE Press (2013)
17. Baumeister, R.F., Leary, M.R.: The need to belong: desire for interpersonal attachments as a fundamental human motivation. Psychol. Bull. **117**(3), 497–529 (1995)
18. Kolbeck, S.: Zur psychometrischen Differenzierbarkeit von sozialen Ängsten und sozialen Defiziten. Eine empirische Studie an nichtklinischen und klinischen Stichproben. Dissertation (2008)
19. Leary, M.R., Dobbins, S.E.: Social anxiety, sexual behavior, and contraceptive use. J. Pers. Soc. Psychol. **45**(6), 1347–1354 (1983)
20. Suzuki, T., Yamada, S., Kanda, T., Nomura, T.: Influence of social avoidance and distress on people's preferences for robots as daily life communication partners. In: Conference Proceedings New Friends 2015 (2015)
21. Syrdal, D.S., Dautenhahn, K., Koay, K.L., Walters, M.L.: The negative attitudes towards robots scale and reactions to robot behaviour in a live human-robot interaction study. Adaptive and Emergent Behaviour and Complex Systems (2009)
22. Nomura, T., Suzuki, T., Kanda, T., Kato, K.: Measurement of negative attitudes toward robots. Interact. Stud. **7**(3), 437–454 (2006)
23. Nomura, T., Shintani, T., Fujii, K., Hokabe, K.: Experimental investigation of relationships between anxiety, negative attitudes, and allowable distance of robots. In: Chamonix, F. (ed.) Proceedings of the 2nd IASTED International Conference on Human Computer Interaction. ACTA Press (2007)
24. Marelich, W.D., Lundquist, J.: Motivations for sexual intimacy: Development of a needs-based sexual intimacy scale. Int. J. Sex. Health **20**(3), 177–186 (2008)
25. Neave, N., Jackson, R., Saxton, T., Hönekopp, J.: The influence of anthropomorphic tendencies on human hoarding behaviours. Pers. Individ. Differ. **72**, 214–219 (2015)
26. Russel, D., Peplau, L.A., Cutrona, C.E.: The revised UCLA Loneliness Scale: Concurrent and discriminant validity evidence. J. Pers. Soc. Psychol. **39**(3), 472–480 (1980)

27. Krämer, N.C., Hoffmann, L., Fuchslocher, A., Eimler, S.C., Szczuka, J.M., Brand, M.: Do i need to belong? development of a scale for measuring the need to belong and its predictive value for media usage. Paper Presented at the Annual Conference of the International Communication Association (ICA), 17–21 June 2013, London, Great Britain (2013)
28. Rosenthal-von der Pütten, A.: Uncannily Human. Empirical Investigation of the Uncanny Valley Phenomenon. Dissertation (2014)

The Cyborg Mermaid (or: How Technè Can Help the Misfits Fit in)

Martine Mussies[✉] and Emiel Maliepaard

Department of Human Geography, Radboud University, Nijmegen, Netherlands
martinemussies@gmail.com, e.maliepaard1@gmail.com

Abstract. In feminist studies, the figure of the mermaid has long been regarded as flawed, disabled and less-than-human. Her theoretical counterpart in that respect would be the cyborg, an image used to show that with the help of robotics, humankind could be larger than life. So, what would happen if we could combine those two images and apply them to create "super love" more-than-human relationships? This article explores the possibilities of technology for "mermaids", people who normally fall outside the norm, to satisfy human desires in a new way. Two case studies will be presented, first we will look at people who identify as having ASD and after that we will look at people who have BDSM-oriented desires. We shortly discuss the added value of practice theory for exploring how people are altered by technè.

Keywords: Mermaid · Cyborg · More-than-human · Practice theory · Autism · BDSM · Hug machine · Pegging

1 Introduction and Backgrounds

1.1 Cyborgs

Half-robot, half-human. The image of the cyborg goes back a long time. As early as 1843, Edgar Allan Poe described a man with extensive prostheses [1]. But its name, "cyborg", was first coined over a century later, in 1960, by Manfred Clynes and Nathan S. Kline, as an abbreviation for "cybernetic organism" [2]. As Cecilia Åsberg explains, this cyborg as described by Clynes and Kline is "the strange product of double fertilization by two fathers, sprouted from the neo-colonial sciences and the militarism of the superpowers during the Cold War between East and West" [3]. Their far-reaching visions of beings with both organic and biomechatronic body parts were soon echoed in popular culture. Popular examples of cyborgs are Darth Vader, Inspector Gadget, the

The paper is a co-production from Martine Mussies and Emiel Maliepaard. Martine had a substantial larger role on the conceptualization of the cyborg, mermaid, and cyborg mermaid and the first case study, whereas Emiel had a role in the reflection and second case study. Additionally, Martine presented our paper at the Second International Congress of Love and Sex with Robots (19-20 December 2016 at Goldsmith University, London).

© Springer International Publishing AG 2017
A.D. Cheok et al. (Eds.): LSR 2016, LNAI 10237, pp. 84–96, 2017.
DOI: 10.1007/978-3-319-57738-8_8

Borg, RoboCop, The Terminator, the Daleks from Dr. Who and the Replicants from Blade Runner. But the cyborg is both virtual and real, as Haraway explains [4, 5]. Nowadays, the idea of the cyborg can be found all around us, in medicine (think about pace makers), in the military (DARPA), in sports (Paralympic Games) and in the so-called "disability studies". Take for example the cyborgization in critical deaf studies. In her article "Do Androids Dream of Electric Speech: The Construction of Cochlear Implant Identity on American Television and the New Deaf Cyborg", Pamela J. Kincheloe discusses the representation of the cochlear implant in media and popular culture as a case study for present and future responses to human alteration and enhancement [6]. Joseph Michael Valente describes cyborgization as an attempt to codify "normalization" through cochlear implantation in young deaf children [7]. Drawing from Paddy Ladd's work on Deaf epistemology and Donna Haraway's Cyborg ontology, Valente takes the concept of the cyborg to agitate constructions of cyborg perfection.

During the panel discussion on the first day of "Love and Sex with Robots 2016", it became clear that it is very hard to define the creature of the cyborg. For this paper, I (Martine) would like to suggest a model, that acknowledges three stages in the process of cyborgization. The first stage would be the cyborg as Dr Genevieve Liveley suggested him/her/they to be: the very basic idea of a human and a "add-on", say: a person wearing glasses. This add-on normalizes, for instance in the example of glasses, the technè "corrects" a person's ability to see, making his vision "normal" and thereby this person just as good, able and human as other humans. Other examples are pace makers, hearing aid etc. The second stage are add-ons that make cyborgs larger than life. A person with blades can run faster than an Olympic runner with legs. The third stage are implants that can be controlled by a third party. For example: a chip under the skin with access to the bank account, Oyster card, or disco. In this paper we are focusing on the second stage as well on the transition from stage 1 to stage 2.

1.2   The Mermaid

The mermaid is only partly human, often half-human, just like the cyborg. But whereas the cyborg is regarded to as being larger than life and an improvement of Mother Nature, the mermaid is often described as flawed, disabled and less-than-human (e.g. [8]). As a symbol for the misfit and the disabled, she struggles with her feelings between longing and belonging and has to change in order to become acceptable as a human being. Andersen's mermaid, for example, cannot reach humans. First literally, because she has no legs. And after that, when this problem is "cured" by a trick or technique – technè in Greek – she figuratively cannot reach humans because she is literally voiceless. To overcome this disability, Disney provides her with yet another technè, so that she can finally be recognized (and marry the prince). As Judith Butler describes in Giving an Account of One's Self, recognition can only take place through a set of social norms [9]. Because the mermaid as a disabled being was not recognized, she was a misfit. Pioneering disability studies scholar Rosemarie Garland-Thomas developed an argument to show how the idea of the misfit manifests itself in three ways. First the disabled body itself, then the vulnerability and dependence and lastly social devaluation [10]. This idea of being a "misfit" surrounded by "real humans", needing to be cured by technè is very present in disability studies. An early account of this idea can be found in the 1908 collection of personal essays by Helen Keller, called "The world I live in" [11]. From the first line of her first essay – "I have just touched my dog" – the deaf-blind Keller makes contact, by sharing her embodied sense of touch (a phenomenological epistemology). But as she cannot speak or make eye contact, she needed writing, a technè, to overcome the distance between herself and the outer world[1].

1.3   A Cyborg Mermaid

While surfing on various about autism as well as about BDSM, it struck me that people often refer to the little mermaid, her feelings and her position as an outcast or misfit in her surroundings. Diving deeper, I even found a whole sub-culture of transgendered woman who identify as "mermaids". Why would people from a subculture choose a mermaid to represent themselves? Amidst all the subjects in the folklore of Europa and the Near East, one of the more common mythical creatures is the mermaid. From Ariel to Undine and from Lorelei to Rusalka, nearly every culture has its own version(s) of the "water woman". Most mermaids seem to lead a tragic life, stuck between longing and belonging, in a space that Homi Bhabha calls "Unhomeliness". Mermaids seem helpless at the mercy of the vagaries of life, tossed about by the choices of male figures in their narrative. We frame the water woman in modern versions (including Andersen's) as a tragic figure, often a victim of love, often relegated to the sea. This image of the mermaid is apparently so strongly rooted that it is even used by feminist scholars like Dorothy Dinnerstein. But does the mermaid have to be a victim of her fate?

I think not. It is no coincidence that one of the attributes of the mermaid is the mirror (which has also led to the Christian connection with vanity), as the image of the mermaid has metamorphosed to mirror the context in which it occurs. Hans Christian Andersen wrote a Victorian and Christian morality tale, in which he could articulate his bi-romantic longings. With the rise of children's films the mermaid became a child/teen heroine (sometimes played by a real life heroine, as in the Dutch mermaid musical with the K3-star). Up till the '90 s, in all her different forms and shapes, is per definition understood as a misfit, as someone who is not an acceptable or correct human being. Even in the dawn of the 21th century, she still often remains a social and/or biological misfit. But by empowering herself with technè she tries to break through societal barriers to become a powerful, and above all, more accepted body. But by empowering herself with technè, the powerless mermaid can become a powerful cyborg. With the advent of games she became a background trope, that is now gaining agency. And in the most recent mermaid game she offers the player a moment of mindfulness, bringing the principles of Soto Zen in practice. Mermaids mirror their context, reflecting developments in society and in our personal experience. But with other attributes than just their mirrors and combs etc., mermaids can become more powerful and mirror the technological developments of the 21th century.

---

[1] In her book *When Species Meet*, Donna Haraway describes the sensation of touching other species as a form of mutual becoming in space and the world rather than an act of affirming the human 'being' [12].

The idea of theoretically challenging the limitations of the body is of course not new. During the last quarter of the 20th century, feminist scholars have problematized the biologic body in roughly four main trends (see for a more thorough discussion [13]). The first angle was the determination, the assumption that your anatomy (sex, race, "disabilities" etc.) determines your fate. The second one was through the lens of scientism, a term used by historians, philosophers, and cultural critics to highlight the possible dangers of lapses towards excessive reductionism in all fields of human knowledge (e.g. [14]). The third way of deconstructing the natural sciences' claims about truth was to problematize the objectification of the body while at the same time criticizing the supposed disembodied nature of scientific reflection [15]. How can we put these ideas into practice? As described above, the process of "cyborgization" is happening all around us. Since the Stone Age, people (or half-humans like Lucy) have overcome their bodily limitations with the use of technology. This is especially valuable for people with so-called disabilities, who can become cyborgs to overcompensate, thus out-competing "natural humans". As mathematical biologist Christian Yates noticed, "in every distance race further than 400 m, the world record times of wheelchair athletes are faster than their able-bodied counterparts" [16]. In this light, we do not change the image of the misfit as Other – a mermaid – but we perceive this Other as being "better" – a cyborg. This leads us to our main question: "What is the impact of the cyborgization on "mermaids" - people who are considered as misfits in our contemporary society?"

2   Case Studies

2.1   Carly Fleischmann and Temple Grandin: Technè and People with ASD

Today's case study for the idea of the cyborg mermaid is the autistic person. My (Martine) personal experiences as a high-functioning Aspergirl, in teaching the piano to autistic children and in researching autism, have ignited in me a wish to critique current views of autism as a condition that renders the autistic as being more or less than human - the first in the case of extraordinary rational and musical abilities, the second in the case of a seemingly defective intelligence and supposedly impaired social abilities. As a liminal figure, the autistic troubles the borders of the "human" such stereotypes presuppose. When I (Martine) was sixteen, I wrote in my diary that "I felt like Ariel with the dinglehopper". In this particular scene, the little mermaid sits on the royal banquet and starts to comb her hair with a fork. It is a very workable solution for tangled up hair and very original. But too far out of the box, which leads to the mermaid being even more "Othered" than with her mutism alone. In her MA thesis on autism autobiographies and the theoretical cyborg figure, Teunie van der Palen states that the critical academic discussion of autistic persons rather advance a post-humanist image of the autistic [17]. As she describes it, the post-human is both what comes after the human, in terms of its incorporation of technology, and what comes after the liberal humanist subject, in terms of normative rationality, empathy, independence and self-hood. Thus the autistic is an example of both: she uses technologies to organize her world, to recognize faces and to produce language and so on. In that sense, she already is a cyborgian creature. To explore what this means, after a general description of ASD – Autism

Spectre Disorders – we will take a look at how technè has improved the lives of two successful female autistic authors: Carly Fleischmann and Temple Grandin.

Under the DSM-5, Autism Spectrum Disorder (ASD) is characterized by persistent deficits in social communication and interaction across multiple contexts, as well as restricted, repetitive patterns of behavior, interests, or activities. But as Hannah Ebben describes in her MA-thesis, "[i]n terms of just the word and not the assemblage of symptoms that it signifies, autism is a concept that has been used to define deviant behavior as well as identity categories in the Western world for the past 70 years" [18]. But as she continues to explain, the term "autism" is even older. The word was first coined by Swiss psychiatrist Eugen Bleuler in 1911. He used this variation on the Old Greek word "autos" to describe (schizophrenic?) people who lived enclosed in their own world [19, 20]. About 30 years later, two Austrian psychoanalysts independently followed in his footsteps, Leo Kanner used the word autism as a defect in relating to other people and a preoccupation [21], while Hans Asperger characterized his "little professors", the talented children who lived in a highly individualized and intellectual world [22]. This view of a world of one's own is recognized by many autistic persons. In their definition of autism, the British National Autism Society writes that it "affects how a person communicates with and relates to other people, and how they experience the world around them." Autistic persons are often referred to as Other, which has led to media representations of them as being non-human (alien, robot, computer), puzzles (many organizations about autism have puzzle pieces in their logo's) and "spatially away" (from another planet, being locked up, traveling through/breaking through autism etc.). Because they often have troubles fitting in, the main struggles for the autistic frequently lie in making appropriate contact with the outside world. A desire which is often hard to fulfill. Or as Disney's little mermaid sings "Wish I could be – part of your world".

On her website, Carly writes: "I am not able to talk out of my mouth, however I have found another way to communicate by spelling on my computer. (and yes that is me typing on the computer by myself)" [23]. With her computer, Carly crosses the boundaries of her autism, making her more 'human,' as Carly Fleischmann's sister remarks (Fleischmann and Fleischmann 172). As a cyborg, she even works as a journalist, writing books and articles, and interviewing people on her own YouTube Channel: Speechless with Carly Fleischmann. Of course, this public voice makes her very powerful. Carly openly writes about her desires when growing up. Not only did she crave friendships, but she also took pleasure in flirting with boys [24]. For the nonverbal woman with autism, or: mermaid, those desires became reality with the help of robotics, leading her father to note: "Unable to feel or share emotions? Nothing could be further from the truth" (277). In a way, with her shift from mermaid to cyborg, robotics empowered Carly by giving her access to new forms of love. It fulfilled her desires in terms of human contact and communication. The same goes for Temple Grandin (1947), an American professor of animal science at Colorado State University with autism. While she was attending college, Temple invented a therapeutic, stress-relieving device, now known as the "hug machine". This hug machine, also described as a hug box, a squeeze machine, or a squeeze box, is a deep-pressure device designed to calm hypersensitive persons, usually individuals with autism spectrum disorders [25]. People with ASD often experience problems in both social interactions and sensitivity to sensory stimulation, often making it uncomfortable or impractical for them to turn to other human beings for comfort. The hug machine can help them, so that by becoming more cyborg, there become less stressed as well as less dependent on other people, which gives them an advance. Just as Carly, Temple thus uses robotics to empower herself, which could be symbolically described as a shift from mermaid to cyborg.

2.2 Technè in Sexual Practices: BDSM and Kink

The second case study is the person with BDSM-orientated desires. As a research assistant for Manuela Alizadeh, I (Martine) interviewed many "kinky" people about their experiences of pain. What struck me is that many participants said that they used pain as a way to establish contact, just like the little mermaid used it, when she walked on knives and had her tongue cut off. Pain – whether it be inflicted by or upon the respondent – becomes technè; a means, tool or by-product in the crossing of the boundaries between the self and the Other. For this desire, the respondents call themselves kinky. But what exactly is "kinky"? Merriam-Webster gives "1: closely twisted or curled, 2: relating to, having, or appealing to unconventional tastes especially in sex; also: sexually deviant 3: outlandish, far-out." of which we obviously need the second one. But this strikes me as being a very extern and functional definition. What does it mean for a person to be kinky? That he or she has sexually loaded desires that are separate from the prevailing norm, but that one longs to see satisfied for a sense of happiness and/or meaning. Thus setting the kinky person apart as an outsider, a misfit in the usual standard. One respondent said that she felt like a "creep", because "pain is healing for me. Addictive. A whirl in which I feel stronger." But there is nothing creepy about this hormonal effect, in the contrary, this has been known for a long time. There are Japanese traditions in which monks slap their pupils, not to punish them, but to deliver the surge of adrenaline that comes with such a pain stimulus and can help in concentration and focus. Thus, it is the social context that makes kinky people "other".

Under the DSM-5, sexual sadism and sexual masochism are included as paraphilia, in the category "algolagnistic disorders" – derived from the Greek words algos (pain) and lagneia (lust). These two conditions characterized by "abnormal" sexual desires are part of the spectrum of BDSM. BDSM is defined as sexual behavior in which pleasure is experienced by pain and this creates a psychological or sexual satisfaction [26]. The abbreviation BDSM refers to three predominant concepts: Bondage and Discipline (B&D), Dominance and Submission (D&S), and Sadism and Masochism (S&M). While these concepts are related to each other, every individual will make a choice between them individually, or a combination of them based on their personal preference, to integrate them into their sexual activities [27]. Thus, a person can play a dominant role, a submissive role or a switch roll, depending on the occasion [28]. The most common activities within BDSM include role-playing, bondage, fetish, and spanking [29]. Several studies indicate the number of people participating in BDSM. A study by Masters, Johnson and Kolodny shows that about 10% of the North American population regularly participates in BDSM [30]. Kolmes, Stock and Moser conclude that fourteen percent of men and eleven percent of women participate in any form of BDSM [26]. In other research, 50% of the respondents indicated to experience sexual excitement with biting [26]. Additionally, about 65% the respondents fantasizes about being tied up and 62% fantasizes about tying up their partner [31]. Despite these large numbers, BDSM is still associated with a social stigma. It is often thought that BDSM participants are psychologically unhealthy and participating in BDSM is often seen as perverse [32–34]. Due to this stigma, respondents often kept their desires to themselves and away from public spheres and places.

The BDSM scene is a versatile community consisting of many different preferences, roles, activities, and practices. Nevertheless, we can focus on the position of non-human bodies ("external prostheses") in the different practices that consist BDSM and kink practices (e.g. strap-on dildos, whips, chains, virtual reality Healslut or vacuum beds). For instance, a practice known as pegging (a person penetrates another person's anus with a strap-on dildo) involves a human-technè interaction to increase pleasure during sexual practices. While an obvious end could be enhancing sexual pleasure, pegging is organized by different orientations towards more specific ends such as domination, stimulation of male genitalia, increasing intimacy, and/or exploring sexual boundaries. These ends are often manifested in the practice itself as a range of moods, emotions, and embodied experiences [35]. The strap-on dildo plays an important role in facilitating the practice of pegging as facilitator of multiple potential sexual doings and sayings.

Pegging is often seen as a collaboration between people and technologies, but we understand this practice as a melting together of technology and human beings to create a more-than-human body, or bodies, and experience(s). The strap-on dildo, in all its different forms and shapes, is not necessarily a substitute of a human penis but an extra genderless bodily option for the one to wear the strap on, which opens up possibilities for new doings, to meet different ends. This extra option is not only there for female on male use, but also for female on female, male on female, and male on male use. Notions to gender performances are not always made by practitioners of sexual practices which include the use of strap-on dildo's (irrespective of the genders involved); A more practical interpretation based upon the use of a strap-on dildo as a practice consisting of specific doings such as carrying a harness, connecting the dildo(s)/vibrator(s), using lubricants, etcetera, is primarily dedicated to enhance psychical and psychological sexual, and possibly relationship, satisfaction by creating atmospheres in which sexual preferences are practiced and experienced. We should not forget the importance of the senses as it does not all come back to functionality but also to the looks, sounds smell, and texture of both the technological addition and the more-than-human entity (e.g. [36]).

The strap-on dildo is just one example of a melting together of technology and human beings to advance sexual practices and create more powerful and intense embodied experiences. Use of technology increases the power, capacities, and capabilities of the direct user, for instance in the flogging practice. In this practice a whip melts together with its users, both physical and psychological, to create a more dominant and powerful human being who is able to give more pain and pleasure to the submissive partner(s). Nevertheless we prefer to speak of creating more powerful and intense embodied experiences and practices instead of speaking of powerful people as technology could also help to restrain someone and render another more powerful such as the use of a leather harness in Bondage and D/s play: The direct user of the harness is constrained whereas it enhances the power and dominance of someone else or others.

Technology is already widely used in sexual practices, sometimes because someone is not able to perform certain practices (empowering powerless mermaids to become powerful cyborgs) but more often to meet other ends. The melting together of technology and human beings in sexual practices creates more effective (read: in meeting certain ends) and powerful sexual practices, and thus, embodied experiences for the direct and indirect users. This does, however, not mean that the mechanisms behind the mermaid are irrelevant in here. In essence, incorporating technè requires ideas about, and experiences of, misfits, people who fit, and how people can fit or function better in society.

3 Reflection

As Verbeek observes "technological development has reached a stage in which technology has started to interfere explicitly with the nature of human beings" [37] (p. 394). Our focus is, in here, on how intimate and sexual practices could potentially be reshaped by technological developments. Instead of focusing on future developments, we explored current use of technè in intimate and sexual practices. Different approaches can be used to better understand the interaction between human bodies and non-human bodies, in particular theories which fit the relational approaches. Examples are actor-network theories [38, 39], more-than-representational theories [40, 41], and theories of practice [35, 42, 43]. One of the main differences between practice theories on the one hand and actor-network theory and more-then-representational theories on the other hand, is the positioning of either practices (theories of practice) or arrangements of bodies (ANT and more-than-representational theories) as building blocks of social life and social order [43]. People position themselves and create meaning by participating in particular practices, including sexual and intimate practices.

Practices not only constitute social life and influences how individuals position themselves in relation to the social world, participating in specific practices also impacts how people experience their lives. Schatzki rejects a body versus mind (or embodiment versus rationality) divide and contends that the human body is the manifold of biological conditions and conditions of life (i.e. body/mind). The former refers to one's physical state of being and the latter to one's being in the world (Zustände). One's being in the world is for a small part natural but foremost the result of social learning and training; conditions of life are "a state of affairs that, in particular circumstances, consists in, is expressed by, particular bodily activities" [35] (p. 34). In other words, how things stand, including in relation with the wider social world, and are going. The emphasis on body/mind and bodies as carriers of practices foregrounds the importance of the human body (including mind) and also raises questions about who is fitting, who is acceptable, and who is acceptable or correct enough to properly participate in our practices? Being a mermaid might be a significant burden for people and people might take up mermaid positions as misfits in our society.

While practice theories focus on human bodies as constituting society alone, it has been recognized that social ideologies, including theories of practice, "treated the social as a domain of human affairs alone" [44] (p. 104) and thus missing the contribution of nonhuman bodies to our contemporary social life. Of course, it would be wrong to ignore how technè can alter the biological conditions of human bodies and what this means for participating in practices and experiencing life. Alteration of biological conditions can happen in multiple ways such as (1) repairing something that is missing and (2) creating a more-than-human body. The former focuses on the mermaids in our society, i.e. how misfits can be corrected to having more acceptable biological conditions. The latter is not specifically focused on mermaids but follows the same logic: to make more acceptable or, perhaps, more correct and functioning human beings[2]. We expect that technè has the potential to increase the number of possible doings and sayings, and enables participation in more practices for "normal" human beings and thus positioning oneself, and being positioned, as a more normal or acceptable human being. As such, by altering the biological conditions, one can increase one's potential to relate and participate.

The question remains, however, how nonhuman bodies contribute to our practices, or how these melt into our practices. Instead of only focusing on bodily doings and sayings as constituents of practices, we need to think about how to incorporate nonhuman bodies in co-creating and sustaining practices. In fact, how can we include technè in our practical understanding of intimate and sexual practices knowing that practices are primary habitual? Reckwitz contends that (1) non-human bodies, or things, are necessary components of many practices and (2) that practices often consists of routinized relating between humans (body/mind) and things [45][3]. In other words, practices are materially interwoven, or materially mediated, arrays of activities [46]. More relevant, however, Reckwitz rightly argues that "carrying out a practice very often means using particular things in a certain way" (emphasis ours) [45] (p. 252). Which things are used and how are they used in sexual and intimate practices? And is the use of technè acceptable or correct within these intimate and sexual practices? In other words, do people accept technè as part of our intimate and sex lives? For instance, Dutch goalkeeper Stefan Postma (ex-Aston Villa and Wolverhampton Wanderers) was involved in a "sex scandal" when his ex-girlfriend leaked a private video in which he was penetrated by her (using a strap-on dildo); a scandal with far-reaching consequences as he was constantly reminded of this video during the rest of his career. At the same time, pegging might be more accepted in certain subgroups of our society such as the BDSM scene. Temple Grandin's hug machine is now used in different therapies to reduce stress and anxiety.

The two above case studies have shown the large potential of existing technè for our sexual and intimate practices and how the hug machine and strap-on dildo are melted into our practices. We are convinced that a hug machine and a strap-on dildo contribute to our social lives and our intimate and sexual practices by being melted into it; it could help to create more acceptable doings and saying for people who are considered as misfits. While

---

[2] Of course, creating more-than-human bodies might result in creating new mermaids in our society: people who are not able to use technè and people who are not willing to incorporate technè in their bodies and lives.

[3] A more recent viewpoint is that non-human bodies not only mediate practices but also actively constitute practices. Inspiration can be drawn from, amongst others, actor-network theory.

we do not believe that technè is meant to make the misfits fit in our society, we understand the potential of technè to reshape our practices, even create new practices, or increase the possibilities for people to participate in more practice; and, thus, provide new opportunities for people to position themselves in relation to the social world. In here we need to focus on how people make use of technè as this manifests people's orientations towards what matters and how things stand. A focus on emotions, moods, state of beings, and actions[4] is vital to understanding people's appreciation of technological innovations.

4 Conclusions

What is the impact of the cyborgization on "mermaids" - people who are considered as mitfits – in our contemporary society? As the examples of Carly Fleischmann and Temple Grandin show, people with ASD could participate in more practices and be less othered by melting together with technè and thus becoming cyborgian creatures. This too is the case for people with BDSM-orientated desires, as the example of pegging shows. Thus, we see robotics as an opportunity to fulfill dreams (including sexual lusts) in situations where it would be biologically difficult or, sometimes, impossible. In the words of Daniel Levy, name giver of this conference: "Many who would otherwise have become social misfits, social outcasts, or even worse will instead be better-balanced human beings" [47] (p. 304). With the image of the cyborg mermaid, the unacceptable can now be made acceptable. The manufacturability (malleability and/or manipulation) of the mermaid can thus be pulled further from the Internet and put in physical forms. This way, robotics can add a valuable contribution to our love lives by making it both better and more diverse. Discussions on teledildonics [48], however, show that changes to our love lives require time before being understood as acceptable additions, or, preferably, improvements to our biological conditions and our sexual and intimate practices.

When we avoid the human-technology divide and bring forward a dialectic and inclusive approach to human, more-than-human (or semi-human), and non-human actors, we arrive at a future-now as described by Deleuze and Guattari: "There is no such thing as either man or nature now, only a process that produces the one within the other and couples the machines together. Producing-machines, desiring machines everywhere, schizophrenic machines, all of species life: the self and the non-self, outside and inside, no longer have any meaning whatsoever" [49]. As our paper shows, by incorporating robotics in human sex and love lives, powerless mermaids can become powerful cyborgs.

Acknowledgments. We would like to thank the anonymous reviewers of the Second International Congress of Love and Sex with Robots for their valuable feedback. We are very grateful for the comments and questions from other participants and visitors of the same conference.

---

[4] Actions do not refer to basic doings or saying but to doings and/or sayings in specific circumstances. In other words, bodily doings and sayings which manifest inner expressions such as sensations and triggers.

References

1. Poe, E.A.: The man that was used up. http://librivox.org/the-works-of-edgar-allan-poe-raven-edition-volume-4-by-edgar-allan-poe/
2. Clynes, M.E., Kline, N.S.: Cyborgs and space. http://web.mit.edu/digitalapollo/Documents/Chapter1/cyborgs.pdf
3. Åsberg, C.: Het lichaam als strijdtoneel: De cyborg en feministische visies op de biologie. In: Buikema, R., Van der Tuin, I. (eds.) Gender in Media, Kunst en Cultuur, pp. 53–74. Coutinho, Bussum (2007)
4. Haraway, D.: Simians, Cyborgs, and Women: The Reinvention of Nature. Routledge, London (1991)
5. Haraway, D.: The promises of monsters: a regenerative politics for inappropriate/d others. In: Grossberg, L., Nelson, C., Treichler, P.A. (eds.) Cultural Studies, pp. 295–337. Routledge, New York (1992)
6. Valente, J.M.: Cyborgization: deaf education for young children in the cochlear implantation era. Qual. Inquiry 17(7), 639–652 (2011). doi:10.1177/1077800411414006
7. Kincheloe, P.J.: Do androids dream of electric speech: the construction of cochlear implant identity on American television and the new deaf cyborg. M/C J. 13(3) (2011) http://journal.media-culture.org.au/index.php/mcjournal/article/view/254
8. De Martelaere, P.: Een verlangen naar ontroostbaarheid. http://www.dbnl.org/tekst/mart003verl01_01/mart003verl01_01.pdf
9. Butler, J.: Giving an Account of One's Self. Fortham University Press, New York (2005)
10. Garland-Thomas, R.: Misfits: a feminist materialist disability concept. In: Devlieger, P., Miranda-Galarza, B., Brown, S.E. (eds.) Rethinking Disability: World Perspectives in Culture and Society. Garant uitgevers, Antwerpen (2016)
11. Keller, H.: The world I live in. https://archive.org/details/worldilivein00kellgoog
12. Haraway, D.: When Species Meet. University of Minnesota Press, Minnesota (2008)
13. Mol, A.: "Sekse" en "wetenschap": Een vergelijking met twee onbekenden. In: Boon, L., De Vries, G. (eds.) Wetenschapstheorie: De empirische wending, pp. 97–107. Wolters-Noordhoff, Groningen (1989)
14. Chargaff, I.: In dispraise of reductionism. Bioscience 47(11), 795–797 (1997)
15. Harding, S.: The Science Question in Feminism. Cornwell University Press, London (1986)
16. Yates, A.: Can disabled athletes outcompete able-bodied athletes? https://www.theguardian.com/sport/2016/sep/08/can-disabled-athletes-outcompete-able-bodied-athletes
17. Van der Palen, T.A.: Cyborg autobiography: autism & the posthuman. https://universiteitutrecht.academia.edu/TeunievanderPalen
18. Ebben, H.: In constant encounter with one's environment: presenting counter-metaphors in the study of the discourse of autism and negotiations of space in literature and visual culture. http://theses.ubn.ru.nl/bitstream/handle/123456789/624/18-08-31%20Ebben%20Thesis.pdf?sequence=1
19. Bleuler, E.: Dementia Praecox, oder Gruppe der Schizophrenien. Leipzig (1911)
20. Parnas, J., Bovet, P.: Autism in schizophrenia revisited. Compr. Psychiatry 32, 7–21 (1991). doi:10.1016/0010-440X(91)90065-K
21. Kanner, L.: Autistic disturbances of affective contact. https://simonsfoundation.s3.amazonaws.com/share/071207-leo-kanner-autistic-affective-contact.pdf
22. Asperger, H.: Die "Autistischen Psychopathen" im Kindesalter. http://www.autismus-biberach.com/Asperger_Hans-_Autistischen_Psychopathen.pdf

23. Fleischmann, C.: http://carlysvoice.com/home/
24. Fleischmann, A., Fleischmann, C.: Carly's Voice: Breaking Through Autism. Touchstone, New York City (2012)
25. Grandin, T.: Calming effects of deep touch pressure in patients with autistic disorder, college students, and animals. http://www.grandin.com/inc/squeeze.html
26. Kolmes, K., Stock, W., Moser, C.: Investigating bias in psychotherapy with BDSM clients. J. Homosex. **50**(2), 301–324 (2006). doi:10.1300/J082v50n02_15
27. Haymore, C.: Sadomasochism: the pleasure of pain. Undergrad. J. Psychol. **15**, 50–56 (2002)
28. Wismeijer, A.J., Van Assen, A.L.M.: Psychological characteristics of BDSM practitioners. J. Sex. Med. **10**(8), 1943–1952 (2013). doi:10.1111/jsm.12192
29. Stockwell, F.M., Walker, D.J., Eshleman, J.W.: Measures of implicit and explicit attitudes toward mainstream and BDSM sexual terms using the IRAP and questionnaire with BDSM/fetish and student participants. Psychol. Rec. **60**(2), 307–324 (2010)
30. Masters, W., Johnson, V., Kolodny, R.: Human Sexuality, 2nd edn. Little, Brown, and Company, Boston (1995)
31. Renaud, C.A., Byers, E.S.: Exploring the frequency, diversity, and context of university students' positive and negative sexual cognitions. Can. J. Hum. Sex. **8**(1), 17–30 (1999)
32. Bezreh, T., Weinber, T.S., Edgar, T.: BDSM disclosure and stigma management: identifying opportunities for sex education. Am. J. Sex. Educ. **7**(1), 37–61 (2012). doi:10.1080/15546128.2012.650984
33. Bourdage, J.S., Lee, K., Ashton, M.C., Perry, A.: Big five and HEXACO model personality correlates of sexuality. Pers. Diff. **43**(6), 1506–1516 (2005). doi:10.1016/j.paid.2007.04.008
34. Gosselin, C., Wilson, G.D.: Sexual Variations: Fetishism, Sadomasochism, and Transvestism. Simon & Schuster, New York (1980)
35. Schatzki, T.R.: Social Practices: A Wittgensteinian Approach to Human Activity and the Social, 4th edn. Cambridge University Press, Cambridge (2008)
36. Brown, G.: Ceramics, clothing and other bodies: affective geographies of homoerotic cruising encounters. Soc. Cult. Geogr. **9**(8), 915–932 (2008). doi:10.1080/14649360802441457
37. Verbeek, P.: Cyborg intentionality: rethinking the phenomenology of human–technology relations. Phenomenol. Cognit. Sci. **7**(3), 387–395 (2008). doi:10.1007/s11097-008-9099-x
38. Latour, B.: Reassembling the Social: An Introduction to Actor-Network Theory. Oxford University Press, Oxford (2005)
39. Murdoch, J.: Inhuman/nonhuman/human: actor-network theory and the prospects for a nondualistic and symmetrical perspective on nature and society. Environ. Plan. D Soc. Space **15**, 731–756 (1997)
40. Thrift, N.: Spatial Formations. Sage, Thousand Oaks (1996)
41. Thrift, N.: Non-representational Theory. Routledge, London (2007)
42. Bourdieu, P.: Outline of a Social Theory of Practice (Translation Richard Nice). Cambridge University Press, Cambridge (1977)
43. Schatzki, T.R.: The Site of the Social: A Philosophical Account of the Constitution of Social Life and Change. Pennsylvania State University Press, University Park Philadelphia (2002)
44. Schatzki, T.R.: Wittgenstein and the social context of an individual life. Hist. Hum. Sci. **13**(1), 93–104 (2000). doi:10.1177/09526950022120629
45. Reckwitz, A.: Towards a theory of practice: a development in culturalist theorizing. Eur. J. Soc. Theory **5**(2), 243–263 (2002). doi:10.1177/13684310222225432

46. Schatzki, T.R.: Introduction: practice theory. In: Schatzki, T.R., Knorr Cetina, K., Von Savigny, E. (eds.) The Practice Turn in Contemporary Theory, pp. 1–14. Routledge, London (2001)
47. Levy, D.: Love and Sex with Robots. Harper Perennial, London (2007)
48. McCain, C.: Let's get digital (2016). https://www.1843magazine.com/design/the-daily/lets-get-digital
49. Deleuze, G., Guattari, F.: Capitalisme et schizoprénie 1: L'Anti-Oedipe, p. 2. Editions du Minuit, Paris (1972). (Translated by Helen R. Lane, Robert Hurley, and Mark Seem)

Exploration of Relational Factors and the Likelihood of a Sexual Robotic Experience

Riley Richards[1](✉), Chelsea Coss[2], and Jace Quinn[2]

[1] Department of Communication, University of Wisconsin–Milwaukee, Milwaukee, WI, USA
richa369@uwm.edu
[2] School of Communication, Western Michigan University, Kalamazoo, MI, USA
{Chelsea.b.coss,Jace.quinn}@wmich.edu

Abstract. As technology progresses, robots will become increasingly involved in our everyday lives. Robots are already available for individual purchase and are starting to appear in our homes and offices. Robots specifically built for sexual experiences are presently available on the market. There is no current research on sexual robots or how it will affect our previous, current, and future sexual relationships. This study asked 133 participants to understand what relational factors could contribute to the likelihood of participants having a sexual episode with a robot. Results indicate one is more likely to have a sexual episode with a robot the more sexual fantasies and risky behavior one partakes in. Additionally, one is less likely to have sex with a robot the more they view robots negatively. Findings are discussed with future research directions.

Keywords: Sexual robot · CASA · Lovotics · Human-robot interaction

1 Introduction

Joel Snell [26] was the first academic to publish on the likelihood of sex robots, that he termed "sexbots" (p. 1). According to Levy [18], human-robot relationships will become normal by 2050 and may even exceed that of human-to-human connection. "The idea of robotic companionship is growing stronger. Given sociable robots, and the fact that people already anthropomorphize robots with human-like characteristics, it will be no surprise if people start to feel an attachment to them" [29] (p. 103). Humans are in favor of having a robotic companion as an assistant or servant [5]. Currently, robots are tasked with doing the 'three D's' jobs that are dull, dirty or dangerous [19].

Roxxxy the first female sex robot, and Rocky the first male sex robot was revealed to the public and have been available for purchase since 2010 [12]. These robots are made to look almost human in order to appeal to their audience. Roxxxy is not only 5 feet 7 inches tall, 120 lb but has synthetic skin and artificial intelligence allowing her to learn the likes and dislikes of her owner [13, 14]. Roxxxy is capable of having simple conversations, express love, and feel the touch of her owner with an expansion of possibilities to come via software updates [28].

© Springer International Publishing AG 2017
A.D. Cheok et al. (Eds.): LSR 2016, LNAI 10237, pp. 97–103, 2017.
DOI: 10.1007/978-3-319-57738-8_9

2   Literature Review

2.1   Robots in Today's Society

A robot's social ability allows them to divulge into our society at an alarming rate. "A sociable robot is able to communicate and interact with us, understand, and even relate to us in a personal way. It is a robot that is socially intelligent in a human-like way" [1] (p. 149). Robots have already been accepted into a multitude of societal areas; Roomba a vacuum cleaning robot, Pleo an entertainment robot, KittyCat a robotic pet, Baby Alive a robotic doll, and Paro a therapy robot [8, 10]. Japan is leading the way on robotic production, including sexual robots [19]. As they lead world production in robots, local businesses are capitalizing on this aspect of a future with sex robots. *Doll no Mori* (Forest of Dolls) is a 24/7 doll-escort service in Tokyo, according to the owner, Hajime Kimura, "originally, we were going to run a regular call girl service, but one day while we were surfing the Net we found a business offering love doll deliverers. We decided the labor costs would be cheaper and changed our line of business" [3] (p. 1). However, we know very little (if anything at all) about the potential impact sex robots will have on our romantic relationships. Sex robots are already available and will become more popular, desirable and accessible but because they are still new, the possible impact they will have on our personal relationships is unknown. The unknown impact is the motivation for this current project.

2.2   Computers Are Social Actors

Computers Are Social Actors (CASA) [21] is a theory of social response and explains humans tend to attribute normal social responses to computers and treat them as humans. Previous human-robot interaction tested this assumption on guilt, face threatening [27], attributions of gender [17], and flattery [9]. Humans tend to treat computers with social, sometimes even personal, qualities without thinking about it. The next step in our evolution with computers is to have emotional and even intimate relationships with robots. Technological advancements with robots include the realistic look, feel, and functionality of their structure and appearance. It is believed that by 2050 people will be married to robots [18]. Based on previous research, the following research question is proposed:

RQ: What relational factors contribute to the likelihood of having sex with a robot?

3   Methodology

3.1   Participants

Participants in this study included 133 adults (63 males and 70 females) within the United States. Majority of the participants identified as White (87.2%, $n = 116$), followed by Black or African-American (7.5%, $n = 10$), Asian (4.5%, $n = 6$), and American Indian or Alaska Native (0.8%, $n = 1$). Participants' age ranged from 19 to 67, with a mean age of 36.3 ($SD = 12.09$). The highest level of education obtained was diverse: bachelor's degree

(35.3%, $n = 47$), high school diploma (25.6%, $n = 34$), associate's degree (19.5%, $n = 26$), master's degree (9.8%, $n = 13$), and general education development (GED) (7.5%, $n = 10$). Participants identified prominently as heterosexual (87.2%, $n = 116$) and either married (46.6%, $n = 62$) or in a dating relationship (27.8%, $n = 37$).

3.2 Procedures

To test the research question offered in this study, a nationwide survey was conducted. Data was collected via Amazon.com's Mechanical Turk (mTurk) service. mTurk allows for research to recruit from a diverse pool of potential participants or "workers". Much like a job board, workers see a list of tasks to be performed along with the rate of pay and a short description based on what they are qualified to do, determined by mTurk. Upon securing informed consent, participants responded to the below instruments and a short demographic survey.

3.3 Instruments

Participants were asked to complete a survey examining their own perceptions of their relationship, fear of intimacy, sexual sensations, sexual experiences, sexual fantasies, attitudes toward robots, and likelihood to have sex with a robot.

Relationship Satisfaction. To measure the satisfaction participants felt toward their most recent romantic partner participants responded to Lawrence and Byers' [16] 5-item relationship satisfaction scale. Participants responded to "In general, how would you describe your overall relationship with your current or most recent partner?" in terms of (bad/good, unpleasant/pleasant, negative/positive, unsatisfying/satisfying, and worthless/very valuable). An acceptable reliability was achieved ($M = 28.24$, $SD = 7.57$, $\alpha = .96$).

Sexual Satisfaction. Lawrence and Bryers' [16] sexual satisfaction scale was used to measure the sexual satisfaction participants felt from their most recent romantic relationship. The instrument includes 5-items asses on a series of 7-point bipolar scales. Participants responded to the question "In general, how would you describe your sexual relationship with your current or most recent partner? In terms of (bad/good, unpleasant/pleasant, negative/positive, unsatisfying/satisfying, and worthless/very valuable). An acceptable readability was achieved ($M = 28.56$, $SD = 7.19$, $\alpha = .96$).

Fear of Intimacy. To evaluate participants level of emotional involvement participants responded to Descutner and Thelen [6] fear of intimacy scale. This scale includes 5-item on a 5-point Likert-type scale from 1 (not at all characteristic of me) to 5 (extremely characteristic of me). The scale asked questions like "I have held back my feelings in previous relationships" and "I have done things in previous relationship to keep me from developing closeness". A reliability of $\alpha = .86$ ($M = 12.32$, $SD = 5.03$) was achieved demonstrating acceptable reliability.

Sexual Sensation Seeking. The sexual sensation seeking scale was assessed with a modified version from Gaither and Sellborn [11] to assess participant's sexual behavior based on their current or most recent partner. The instrument included 11-items measured on a 4-point Likert-type scale from 1 (not at all like me) to 4 (very much like me) and made statement like "I like wild "uninhibited" sexual encounters" and "my sexual partners probably think I am a "risk taker". The instrument achieved acceptable reliability ($M = 28.86$, $SD = 6.89$, $\alpha = .87$).

Sex Drive. A 4-item modified version of the Arizona sexual experience scale measured participant's sex drive [20]. The four items included were measured using a 6-point Likert-type scale based on the last week including today and included: "how string is your sex drive?" (extremely strong to no sex drive), "how easily are you sexual aroused (turned on?" (extremely easy to never), "how easily can you reach and orgasm?" (extremely easy to never), and "are your orgasms satisfying?" (extremely satisfying to can't reach orgasm). Items were scored such that higher values represent higher amounts of sex drive. The instrument achieved an acceptable reliability of $\alpha = .84$ ($M = 17.61$, $SD = 3.92$).

Sexual Fantasy. The sexual fantasy scale [15] measured participant's erotic fantasies by 6-items on a 5-point Likert-type scale (never to quite often). The instrument asked questions like "I think about an imaginary lover" and "I imagine that I am having sex with multiple partners simultaneously". The scale achieved acceptable reliability ($M = 15.17$, $SD = 5.71$, $\alpha = .83$).

Negative Attitude Toward Robots. The negative attitude toward robots (NARS) by Nomure, Suzuki, Kanda, and Kato's [22] measures particpants overall attitude toward robots. The instrument includes 14-items assessed on a 7-point Likert-type scale from 1 (strongly disagree) to 7 (strongly agree). The instrument asks questions like "I would feel uneasy if robots really had emotions" and "I would feel paranoid talking to a robot". The instrument achieved an acceptable reliability ($M = 53.33$, $SD = 14.83$, $\alpha = .87$).

Likelihood to have Sex with a Robot. The likelihood to have sex with a robot was measured by the authors' creation of a 10-item 7-point Likert-type scale ranging from extremely unlikely/unaroused to extremely likely/aroused. Sample questions that were asked consisted of "how likely are you to engage in sexual activity with a humanoid robot?" and "how likely would you be to use a sex robot to fulfill any sexual fantasies?". Higher scores represent more likely to have a sexual episode with a robot. An acceptable reliability of .97($M = 34.89$, $SD = 21.20$) was obtained.

4   Results

In order to determine what, if any, relational factors were correlated with the likelihood to have sex with a robot, seven bivariate correlation analyses were conducted. Using the Bonferroni approach to control for Type I error across the seven correlations, a p value of less than or equal to .007($.05/7 = .007$) was required for significance.

Results indicated a significant medium-to-large positive relationship between sexual sensation seeking and likelihood to have sex with a robot (r(133) = .445, $p < .001$). Results indicated a significant medium-to-large positive relationship between fantasy and likelihood to have sex with a robot (r(133) = .494, $p < .001$). Results indicated a significant small-to-medium negative relationship between Negative Attitudes Toward Robots and likelihood to have sex with a robot (r(133) = −.234, $p = .003$).

Results indicated no significance between the likelihood to have sex with a robot and relationship satisfaction (r(133) = −.170, $p = .025$), sexual satisfaction (r(133) = −.190, $p = .014$), fear of intimacy (r(133) = .183, $p = .018$), and sex drive (r(133) = −.183, $p = .017$).

5 Discussion

The study examined how relational and sexual satisfaction and attitudes toward robots could possibly be correlated to one's likelihood to have a sexual episode with a robot. A significant positive relationship was found between likelihood to have sex with a robot sexual sensation seeking and sexual fantasy. Simply speaking the more, one seeks out risky sexual behavior and has sexual fantasies the more one is likely to have a sexual episode with a robot. Additionally, a significant negative relationship was found between the likelihood to have sex with a robot and negative attitude toward robots. It is easily assumed if you view robots in a negative way you are less likely to have sex with one.

While the Bonferroni approach to control for a Type I error was utilized, the non-significant results are worth attention. If the standard .05 value was used for significance instead of the .007 used in this study. Significance would have been found between the likelihood to have sex with a robot and relationships satisfaction, sexual satisfaction, fear of intimacy, and sex drive. Future studies should consider interpersonal variables such as these as it relates to future behavior, e.g. livelihood to have sex with a robot.

Due to the future phenomenon of sexual robots and the exploratory nature of the project, it does have limitations. Human-robotic interaction (HRI) and social robotics in society is still growing from the early 2000's, thus potential participants may be unfamiliar with robotics let alone sexual robots. Although it is a potential limitation, it does offer a future research direction to further understand how participants envision a sexual robot. Humanoid robots are increasingly being built for our own benefit or well-being [4]. Additionally, like many survey-based studies, self-identified information was utilized. Although the information questioned in the survey is personal in nature related to sexual content. Participants discussing sexual content usually give socially desirable responses to research, although utilizing web-based surveys minimized this effect [7, 24]. Future research should consider other methodology to cross reference the findings from this study. The field of Lovotics could benefit greatly by forwarding this literature and addressing the limitations.

Additionally, participants were majority Caucasian (87.2%), heterosexual (87.2%) middle-aged ($M = 36.3$), and educated with a higher-level education degree (64.6%). These participants offer an insight into their demographic and future analysis is needed to see if differences exist between cultural and age groups. Beyond demographical issues, it is unknown what participants pictured as a "sex robot" when answering the likelihood to have sex with a robot measurement. Future validation of the scale is needed to continue the current line of research. Furthermore, future research should include a theoretical framework to further understand the motivation and likelihood for future sexual episodes with a robot. However, further exploratory data may be necessary to arrive at a theoretical standpoint. If Levy [18] is correct, and sexual robots and humans will marry 2050, a deeper understanding of the potential impact they will have on our current sexual lives is needed.

References

1. Breazeal, C.: Designing sociable machines. In: Dautenhahn, K., Bond, A., Cañamero, L., Edmonds, B. (eds.) Socially Intelligent Agents: Creating Relationships with Computers and Robots, pp. 149–156. Springer, US (2002)
2. Brooks, R.: Flesh and Machines: How Robots will Change Us. Vintage (2002)
3. Connell, R.: Rent-a-doll blows market wide open. Mainichi Daily News (2004)
4. Cooney, M.D., Nishio, S., Ishiguro, H.: Designing robots for well-being: Theoretical background and visual scenes of affectionate play with a small humanoid robot. Lovotics 1(1), 1–9 (2015)
5. Dautenhahn, K., Woods, S., Kaouri, C., Walters, M.L., Koay, K.L., Werry, I.: What is a robot companion-friend, assistant or butler? Intelligent Robots and Systems, pp. 1192–1197 (2005). doi:10.1109/IROS.2005.1545189
6. Descutner, C.J., Thelen, M.H.: Development and validation of a fear-of-intimacy scale. Psychol. Assess. J. Consult. Clin. Psychol. 3(2), 218–225 (1991)
7. Dillman, D.A.: Mail and internet surveys: The tailored design method, vol. 2. Wiley, New York (2000)
8. Fernaeus, Y., Håkansson, M., Jacobsson, M., Ljungblad, S.: How do you play with a robotic toy animal?: A long-term study of pleo. In: Proceedings of the 9th International Conference on interaction Design and Children, pp. 39–48 (2010). doi:10.1145/1810543.1810549
9. Fogg, B.J., Nass, C.: Silicon sycophants: the effects of computers that flatter. Int. J. Hum Comput Stud. 46, 551–561 (1997). doi:10.1006/ijhc.1996.0104
10. Forlizzi, J., DiSalvo, C.: Service robots in the domestic environment: a study of the roomba vacuum in the home. In: Proceedings of the 1st ACM SIGCHI/SIGART Conference on Human-Robot Interaction, pp. 258–265 (2006). doi:10.1145/1121241.1121286
11. Gaither, G.A., Sellbom, M.: The sexual sensation seeking scale: reliablity and validity within a heterosexual college student sample. J. Pers. Assess. 81(2), 157–167 (2003). doi:10.1207/S15327752JPA8102_07
12. Griggs, B.: Inventor unveils $7,000 talking sex robot. CNN, 1 February 2010. http://www.cnn.com/2010/TECH/02/01/sex.robot/
13. Heater, B.: Roxxxy the 'sex robot' debuts at AVN porn show. PC Magazine, 9 January 2010. http://www.pcmag.com/article2/0,2817,2357928,00.asp
14. Hough, A.: Foxy 'Roxxxy': World's first 'sex robot' can talk about football. The Telegraph, 11 January 2010. http://www.telegraph.co.uk/news/newstopics/howaboutthat/6963383/Foxy-Roxxxy-worlds-first-sex-robot-can-talk-about-football.html
15. Knafo, D., Jaffe, Y.: Sexual fantasizing in males and females. J. Res. Pers. 18(4), 451–462 (1984)
16. Lawrence, K., Byers, E.S.: Sexual satisfaction in long-term heterosexual relationships: The interpersonal exchange model of sexual satisfaction. Personal Relationships 2(2), 267–285 (1995)

17. Lee, E. J., Nass, C., Brave, S.: Can computer-generated speech have gender?: An experimental test of gender stereotypes. In: Computer-Human Interaction (CHI) Conference, The Hague, Amsterdam (2000)
18. Levy, D.: Love and Sex with Robots. HarperCollins Publishers, New York (2009)
19. Lin, P., Abney, K., Bekey, G.A.: Robot Ethics: The Ethical and Social Implications of Robotics. MIT press, Cambridge (2011)
20. McGahuey, C.A., Gelenberg, A.J., Laukes, C.A., Moreno, F.A., Delgado, P.L., McKnight, K.M., Manber, R.: The Arizona Sexual Experience Scale (ASEX): reliability and validity. J. Sex Marital Ther. **26**(1), 25–40 (2000). doi:10.1080/009262300278623
21. Nass, C.I., Steuer, J.S., Tauber, S., Reeder, H.: Anthropomorphism, agency, and ethiopia: computers as social actors. In: Ashlund, S., Mullet, K., Henderson, A., Hollnagel, E., White, T. (eds.) Proceedings of the Computer-Human Interaction (CHI 1993) Conference Companion on Human Factors in Computing Systems, pp. 111–112. Association of Computing Machinery, New York (1993). doi:10.1145/259964.260137
22. Nomura, T., Kanda, T., Suzuki, T.: Experimental investigation into influence of negative attitudes toward robots on human–robot interaction. AI & Soc. **20**(2), 138–150 (2006). doi: 10.1007/s00146-005-0012-7
23. Nomura, S., Tek, K., Samani, H., Godage, I., Narangoda, M., Cheok, A.: Fesibility of social interfaces based on tactile senses for caring communication. In: The 8th International Workshop on Social Intelligence Design – SID 2009 (2009)
24. Orbuch, T., Harvey, J.H.: Methodological and conceptual issues in the study of the sexuality in close relationships. In: McKinney, K., Sprecher, S. (eds.) Sexuality in Close Relationships, pp. 9–24. Lawrence Erlbaum, Hillsdale (1991)
25. Samani, H.A.: Lovotics: love + robotics, sentimental robot with affective artificial intelligence (Doctoral dissertation). National University of Singapore (2011)
26. Snell, J.C.: Impacts of robotic sex. The Futurist **31**(4), 32 (1997)
27. Stoll, B., Edwards, C., Edwards, A.: Why aren't you a sassy little thing: the effects of robot-enacted guilt trips on credibility and consensus in a negotiation. Communication Studies, pp. 1–18 (2016). doi:10.1080/10510974.2016.1215339
28. Svennson, P.: Roxxxy sex robot (photos): world's first robot girlfriend' can do more than chat. Huffington Post, 18 March 2010. http://www.huffingtonpost.com/2010/01/10/roxxxy-sex-robot-photo-wo_n_417976.html
29. Young, J.E., Hawkins, R., Sharlin, E., Igarashi, T.: Toward acceptable domestic robots: applying insights from social psychology. Int. J. Soc. Robot **1**(1), 95–108 (2009)

The Impact of a Humanlike Communication Medium on the Development of Intimate Human Relationship

Nobuhiro Jinnai[2(✉)], Hidenobu Sumioka[1],
Takashi Minato[1], and Hiroshi Ishiguro[1,2]

[1] Advanced Telecommunication Research Institute International, 2-2-2 Hikaridai,
Seika-cho, Soraku-gun, Kyoto 619-0288, Japan
{sumioka,minato}@atr.jp
[2] Graduated School of Engineering Science, Osaka University, Osaka, Japan
jinnai.nobuhiro@irl.sys.es.osaka-u.ac.jp, ishiguro@sys.es.osaka-u.ac.jp

Abstract. In this paper, we reports how a humanlike communication medium affects the development of human relationship. We examined changes in the relationship between persons when they interact with each other through humanlike communication media or mobile phones for about a month. The intimacy of their relationship was evaluated with the amount of self-disclosure. The result shows that a communication medium with humanlike appearance facilitates the development of intimate relationship even when it just has humanlike shape and other functions are the same as standard mobile phones. We also discuss a possible underlying mechanism of this effect from misattribution of a feeling caused by intimate distance with the medium to a conversation partner.

Keywords: Social presence · Mediated social interaction · Human relationship

1 Introduction

Recent advance in ICT has provided diverse ways of communicating and developing personal relationship with others. This enables us to easily find a new friend or partner as well as to keep in touch with friends and family members. On the other hand, researchers have warned that mediated interaction attenuates human relations [6,8,13], compared with face-to-face interaction. One reason is that we do not feel a sense of sharing the same space with conversation partners who are in a distant location in mediated interaction.

We address this problem by using a humanlike robotic avatar representing a distant person as a communication medium since a physical entity allows people to feel a remote person [9]. As shown in the previous studies [15], such media promote good human relationship even when its humanlikeness is minimized. However, no study has been done to investigate how humanlike communication media affect the development of human relationship.

© Springer International Publishing AG 2017
A.D. Cheok et al. (Eds.): LSR 2016, LNAI 10237, pp. 104–114, 2017.
DOI: 10.1007/978-3-319-57738-8_10

In this paper, we examine how people constructs relationship with unfamiliar person when they interact with each other through humanlike communication media or mobile phones for about a month. We report that a humanlike communication medium facilitates the construction of good relationship with unfamiliar person even when it is equivalent to a mobile phone except that it has soft body with humanlike appearance.

2   Related Work

In psychology, some studies reports how people develop intimate relationships with others. Altman and Taylor proposed the social penetration theory [1], which states that the relationship development occurs primarily through self-disclosure, or intentionally revealing personal information such as personal motives, feelings, and thoughts. They reports that through self-disclosure, relationship development moves from superficial layers of exchanges to more intimate ones. This theory was supported by the observational study that as male roommates develop interpersonal relationships, they gradually disclose and express themselves [17].

Other studies criticize social penetration theory and take a different perspective. Berg et al. argue that intimate relationship is developed quickly with initial attraction between strangers rather than gradually [3] and proposed the early differentiation of relatedness theory. They investigated how previously unacquainted university roommates develop intimate relationships from the beginning to the end of a year. The result showed a possibility that the roommates make the decision of whether to room with their mates for an additional year at quite early phase in the relationship [2].

Although there are many studies about the development of intimate in human-human interaction, there is a few study that investigates how the long-term use of mediated communication affect the development of intimate relationship. Especially, no study attempts to investigate the impact of the humanlike features of mediated communication on building intimate relationship.

3   A Handheld Robotic Medium: Elfoid

Elfoid has been developed as a mobile phone that conveys a distant person's presence [5]. Its main feature is its humanlike shape: humanlike head, arms, and legs but no hands and feet. Its skin is fashioned from sponge to resemble and feel like human skin. While the original version of Elfoid was developed as a replacement of a mobile phone, we used a mobile-phone cover in the shape of Elfoid to make all functions equivalent to a mobile phone except for soft body and humanlike appearance (Fig. 1). It has a hole in its breast to make sound from the mobile phone loud and clear. People talk with a conversation partner in a distant place while holding it with hands-free mode.

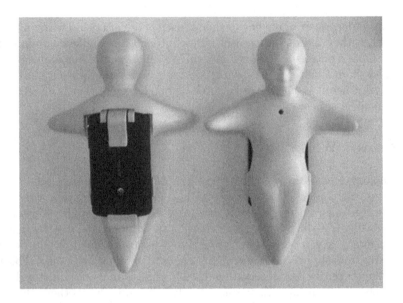

Fig. 1. Elfoid. This version of Elfoid is equal to a mobile-phone cover. We put it on a standard mobile phone.

4 Current Study

We have shown that Elfoid provides stronger feeling of human presence than a device with mechanical appearance for us [14,16]. Previous studies suggest that people get more intimate in face-to-face interaction than in audio-/video-mediated interaction [6,8,13]. We expect that Elfoid enables us to have strong feeling of being together with a conversation partner and help us to get closer thanks to its humanlike features. Therefore, we investigate the effect of human-like communication media on human relationship in long-term use, hypothesizing that the interaction mediated with Elfoid facilitates good relationship compared with the interaction through a mobile phone.

5 Experiment

5.1 Participants

Twelve people participated in the experiment (4 males, mean age 22.5 years). We separated them into two groups each of which consists of 3 pairs (a male-female pair and two female-female pairs): the Elfoid group, whose pairs talked with each other through Elfoid in separate rooms, and the Phone group, whose pairs talked through mobile phones (Fig. 2). It was confirmed that each pair did not know each other.

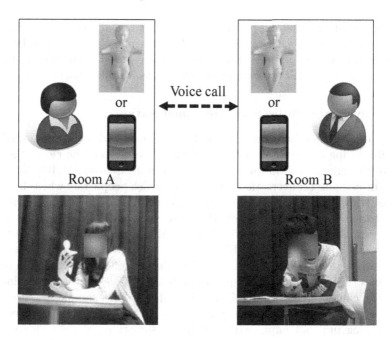

Fig. 2. An experimental setting

5.2 Procedure

The participants had 10 min conversation with the same partner twice a week. In total, they had ten conversations (one hundred min.) for about one month. Each conversation was recorded. We asked them to call each other by their family name. In the conversation, asking the partner's first name was forbidden because knowing full name enables the participants to find their partners in SNS and to keep in touch over the internet. The participants were also not allowed to ask religious belief and political affiliation because biased impression against such information influences building human relationship. The conversation topic was not limited except for these topics. The participants were not allowed to meet each other during the experiment. They also answered SSI described below before or after experiments.

5.3 Assessment of Social Skills

We evaluated social skills of each participant with Social Skills Inventory (SSI) [11] because they affect the construction of close relationship with other persons. The SSI has seven factors: emotional expressivity, emotional sensitivity, emotional control, social expressivity, social sensitivity, social control, and social manipulation. Among them, social expressivity refers to general verbal speaking skill and an ability to engage others in social interaction [11]. A person who has a good skill of social expressivity likes having social interaction and initiates conversation with other people. This skill is primary important to facilitate conversation in this experiment. Therefore, we measured participant's score of social expressivity in SSI to evaluate communication skill of participants.

5.4 Analysis of Self-disclosure in Conversation

We evaluated the development of intimate relationship with the amount of self-disclosure during conversation since researchers argue that the closer the relationship, the greater the intimacy or depth of self-disclosure [1,10]. Niwa and Maruno investigated conversation topics about which people talk when they want others to know themselves and developed a questionnaire for the assessment of the depth of self-disclosure. This questionnaire consists of 24 conversation topics, which were answered on a scale from 1 (I do not talk about this topic to a target person at all.) to 7 (I talk about this topic in detail to a target person.), and has high sensitivity for different depths of self-disclosure reflecting four different levels: hobbies (level 1), difficult experiences (level 2), foibles (level 3), and inferior personality characteristics and abilities (level 4) [7]. For example, the first level has seven topics about hobbies: (1) favorites, (2) ways to spend the weekend, (3) something fun that happened recently, (4) something about which you are enthusiastic recently, (5) hobbies, (6) events to which you are looking forward, (7) something that you want to do.

We used this questionnaire to evaluate self-disclosure in conversation. We checked conversation topics with recorded video and determined whether topics presented in the conversation were included into topics in this questionnaire. When the topics were included ones in the questionnaire, they were then judged as topics for self-disclosure. We counted topics for self-disclosure in conversation and used the number of topics for self-disclosure as the amount of self-disclosure to evaluate good relationship in each conversation. The total amount of self-disclosure for each participant was also calculated through all conversations of the participant. We conducted statistical analysis with the standardized values of the amount of self-disclosure for each participant.

6   Result

6.1 Social Expressivity in SSI

The average scores of social expressivity in SSI in Elfoid group and Phone one were 2.88 (SD:0.50) and 3.10 (SD:0.31), respectively. There was no significant difference between two groups for them ($t(5) = -0.81, p = 0.43$). This indicates that participants in both groups had a similar level of social skills.

6.2 Total Amount of Self-disclosure

Figure 3 shows the averages of the total self-disclosure in both groups. Participants in Elfoid group expressed 17.17 (SD:6.96) self-disclosure while ones in

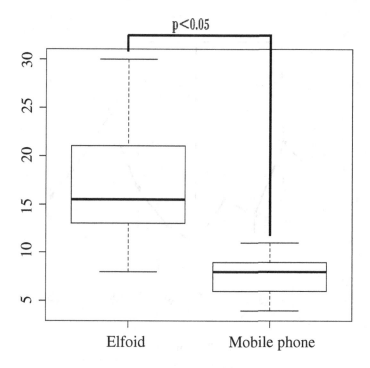

Fig. 3. The average of total amount of self-disclosure

Phone group showed 7.67 (SD:2.21) self-disclosure in Phone group. The result with Welch's t-test showed that participants in Elfoid group showed more self-disclosure than ones in Phone group $(t(5) = 2.91, p < .05)$.

6.3 Changes of the Amount of Self-disclosure

Figure 4a and b show the averages and standard deviations of the amount of self-disclosure in each conversation session in Elfoid group and Phone group, respectively. One-sample t-test for each conversation session showed that participants in Elfoid group express less self-disclosure on fifth session than on other sessions $(t(5) = -5.88, p < .01)$ and ones in Phone group express less self-disclosure on seventh session than on other sessions $(t(5) = -5.01, p < .01)$. We also found that participants in Elfoid group show more self-disclosure on second session $(t(5) = 3.01, p < .05)$ and eighth session $(t(5) = 3.34, p < .05)$ than on fifth session. In Phone group, participants showed more self-disclosure on fourth session than on seven session $(t(5) = 3.19, p < .05)$.

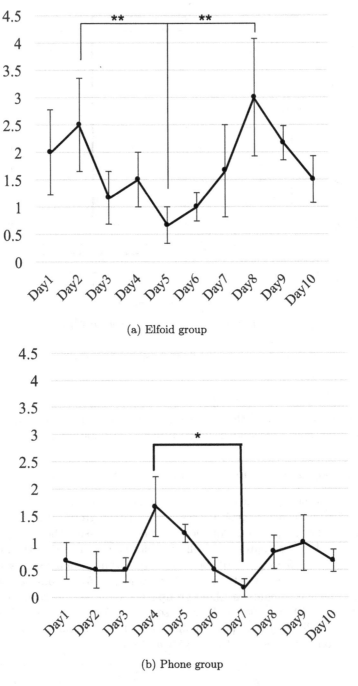

(a) Elfoid group

(b) Phone group

Fig. 4. The changes of the amount of self-disclosure in Elfoid and Phone groups. The values presented in the figures are not standardized. **: $p < .01$, *: $p < .05$.

7   Discussion

The results showed that a communication medium with humanlike appearance increases the amount of self-disclosure even when it just has humanlike shape and soft body and other functions are the same as standard mobile phones. This supports our hypothesis that the interaction mediated with humanlike communication media facilitate intimate relationship compared with the interaction through typical communication media because self-disclosure is an index of intimacy [1,10].

Why did humanlike features cause the significant difference? As one possible reason, we point out that the situation of talking through Elfoid with holding it is similar to face-to-face intimate interaction. Research on proxemics has suggested that interpersonal distance represents human relationship [4]. Interestingly, while participants in Phone group put their mobile phones on the desk, five out of six participants in Elfoid group kept holding Elfoid through the experiment and the rest one also kept holding it after the seventh session. Especially, two participants often showed touching behavior to Elfoid: stroking, pinching, or holding its body, arms, legs, or head (Fig. 5). Therefore, people who used Elfoid might misattribute an affinity with Elfoid to their conversation partners because Elfoid is within their intimate distance. We will investigate whether such misattribution to the partner happens or not as a future work.

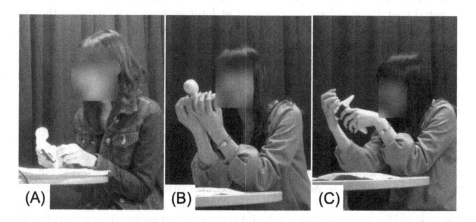

Fig. 5. Touching behavior to Elfoid. Participants showed (A) stroking its body, (B) stroking its arms, and (C) holding its head.

Another possibility is that participants in Elfoid group had a strong feeling of being together with their conversation partners. Previous studies report that people feel as if they were together with conversation partners who are actually in a distant place when they communicate with a humanlike communication medium as a proxy of the partners [12,15]. Actually, some participants in Elfoid

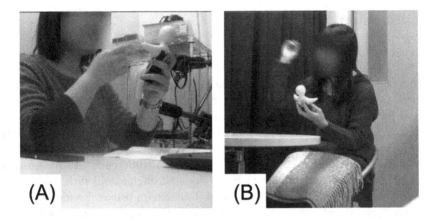

Fig. 6. Gesture toward Elfoid. (A) pointing gesture to Elfoid. (B) throwing motion

group looked like dealing with Elfoid as a human. For example, one participant laughed and showed pointing gesture toward Elfoid while listening to her partner's talk at seventh and eighth conversation sessions. Another showed a throwing motion while her talking at ninth session (Fig. 6). Since these behaviors were not observed in Phone group, probably Elfoid's humanlike features elicit a feeling of face-to-face interaction with a conversation partner. It should be noted that these behaviors appeared at later sessions. This implies that as people communicate with a conversation partner through a humanlike device, they gradually feel as if the device was the partner.

Interestingly, we also found that intimate relationship might develops with increase-decrease cycle of the amount of disclosure: once people disclose and express themselves to an unacquainted person in conversation, they decrease self-disclosure for a while and then they again increase self-disclosure. In Elfoid group, the amount of self-disclosure declined between second session and fifth one and then rose between fifth session and eighth one. We infer that this is because people talk about information about themselves for several conversations when they provide it for each other. In fact, after a male participant talked about his travel plan at second session, he and his conversation partner talked together about the detailed plan at fourth session. This increase-decrease cycle was not observed in Phone group. But, we found the significant decline between at fourth session and seventh one that seems correspond to the decline in Elfoid group, which starts from the second session. We speculate that a Elfoid accelerates the increase-decrease cycle and will investigate whether a phase of increase appear in Phone group or not when participants have more conversations in the future.

We did not find any results that support the social penetration theory. The amount of participant's self-disclosure did not gradually increase. Instead, we found the increase-decrease cycle of self-disclosure. This might be because studies on the social penetration theory focus on the development of intimate relationship during much longer term such as several months or one year and the pairs who have much more opportunities to meet each other such as roommates [17]. Therefore, we infer that the amount of self-disclosure gradually increase with repetition of the cycle for longer term.

Our results showed that a humanlike communication medium increased self-disclosure between strangers for about a month after they meet. The early differentiation of relatedness theory implies that such a medium facilitates the construction of intimate relationship between them. As suggested in the theory, the initial attraction of a conversation partner is an important factor to construct intimate relationship quickly. Therefore, pairs in Elfoid group probably had more intimate relationship than ones in Phone group even after the experiment finished although we did not follow up their relationship. The further investigation is required as a future work.

8   Conclusion

In this paper, we showed that long-term use of a humanlike communication medium, called Elfoid, increased self-disclosure in conversation with an unacquainted person, compared with a standard mobile phone. Furthermore, we also found that such a medium could accelerate the process of constructing intimate relationship with the person. Our observation suggested the possibility that these results were caused by humanlike features of Elfoid that created the situation similar to face-to-face intimate interaction. Our current study has several limitations. An obvious limitation is that sample size is relatively small. We have to verify our result with larger sample size. The movement of Elfoid will enhance a stronger feeling of being together with a remote person although we used Elfoid that does not have any actuators. Our study increases understanding of the effect of humanlike communication media on human relationship and will provide one of several problems in telecommunication for us.

Acknowledgements. This work has been supported by JST CREST research promotion program "Creation of Human-Harmonized Information Technology for Convivial Society" Research Area, JSPS KAKENHI (Grant Number: JP26560018 and JP26330240), and JST, ERATO, ISHIGURO symbiotic Human-Robot Interaction Project.

References

1. Altman, I., Taylor, D.A.: Social Penetration: The Development of Interpersonal Relationships. Rinehart & Winston, Holt (1973)
2. Berg, J.H.: Development of friendship between roommates. J. Pers. Soc. Psychol. **46**(2), 346 (1984)
3. Berg, J.H., Clark, M.S.: Differences in social exchange between intimate, other relationships: gradually evolving or quickly apparent? In: Derlega, V.J., Winstead, B.A. (eds.) Friendship and Social Interaction, pp. 101–128. Springer, New York (1986)
4. Hall, E.T.: The Hidden Dimension. Doubleday & Co., Garden City (1966)

5. Minato, T., Sumioka, H., Nishio, S., Ishiguro, H.: Studying the influence of hand-held robotic media on social communications. In: RO-MAN Workshop on Social Robotic Telepresence, pp. 15–16 (2012)
6. Murase, K.: Distance counseling, counseling approaches, and state anxiety. Jpn. J. Pers. **14**(3), 324–326 (2006) (in Japanese)
7. Niwa, S., Maruno, S.: Development of a scale to assess the depth of self-disclosure. Jpn. J. Pers. **18**(3), 196–209 (2010) (in Japanese)
8. O'Malley, C., Langton, S., Anderson, A., Doherty-Sneddon, G., Bruce, V.: Comparison of face-to-face and video-mediated interaction. Interact. Comput. **8**(2), 177–192 (1996)
9. Paulos, E., Canny, J.: Social tele-embodiment: understanding presence. Auton. Robots **11**(1), 87–95 (2001)
10. Reis, T.H., Shaver, P., et al.: Intimacy as an interpersonal process. Handb. Pers. Relat. **24**(3), 367–389 (1988)
11. Riggio, R.E.: Assessment of basic social skills. J. Pers. Soc. Psychol. **51**(3), 649 (1986)
12. Sakamoto, D., Kanda, T., Ono, T., Ishiguro, H., Hagita, N.: Android as a telecommunication medium with a human-like presence. In: 2nd ACM/IEEE International Conference on Human-Robot Interaction (HRI), pp. 193–200. IEEE (2007)
13. Stephenson, G.M., Ayling, K., Rutter, D.R.: The role of visual communication in social exchange. Brit. J. Soc. Clin. Psychol. **15**(2), 113–120 (1976)
14. Sumioka, H., Koda, K., Nishio, S., Minato, T., Ishiguro, H.: Revisiting ancient design of human form for communication avatar: design considerations from chronological development of dogu. In: IEEE International Symposium on Robot and Human Interactive, Communication, pp. 726–731 (2013)
15. Sumioka, H., Nishio, S., Minato, T., Yamazaki, R., Ishiguro, H.: Minimal human design approach for sonzai-kan media: investigation of a feeling of human presence. Cogn. Comput. **6**(4), 760–774 (2014)
16. Tanaka, K., Nakanishi, H., Ishiguro, H.: Physical embodiment can produce robot operator's pseudo presence. Front. ICT **2**(8) (2015). doi:10.3389/fict.2015.00008
17. Taylor, D.A.: Some aspects of the development of interpersonal relationships: social penetration processes. J. Soc. Psychol. **75**, 79–90 (1968)

Kissenger – Development of a Real-Time Internet Kiss Communication Interface for Mobile Phones

Emma Yann Zhang[1,2(✉)], Shogo Nishiguchi[3], Adrian David Cheok[1,2], and Yukihiro Morisawa[4]

[1] Department of Computer Science, City University of London, Northampton Square, London, EC1V 0HB, UK
{Emma.Zhang,Adriancheok}@city.ac.uk
[2] Imagineering Institute, 4 Lebuh Medini Utara, 79200 Iskandar Puteri, Malaysia
{Emma,Adrian}@imagineeringinstitute.org
[3] Intelligent Robotics Laboratory, Osaka University, Yamadaoka, Suita, Osaka 565-0871, Japan
Nishiguchi.shogo@irl.sys.es.osaka-u.ac.jp
[4] Saitama Institute of Technology, Fusaiji, Fukaya, Saitama 369-0203, Japan
morisawayukihiro@sit.ac.jp

Abstract. A real-time bilateral kiss communication interface is developed for transmitting multisensory kissing sensations over the Internet using mobile phones. Kissenger consists of a plugin haptic device that attaches to a mobile phone via the audio jack and a mobile application that connects to the device and sends real-time data stream over the Internet. The device uses an array of linear actuators to generate haptic stimulations on the human lips and force sensors to measure the force output. Bilateral force-feedback control is used to synchronise the forces on both sides of the system. The aim is to provide an intimate communication channel for couples and families to physically interact with each other in order to maintain close relationships even at a distance. The stimulation of other sensory modalities such as taste and smell are discussed to provide a full multisensory communication experience.

1 Introduction

Many people nowadays are living apart from their friends and families and their communications are limited to voice or video calls and sending text messages with their mobile phones. Although these communication methods are sufficient for keeping in touch and sharing information about their everyday life, touching or kissing our loved ones over the Internet remains to be a challenge yet to be addressed by most communication systems. This is perhaps due to a lack of understanding of the significance of physical interaction in improving relationship qualities or a reluctance to approach such a sensitive or private topic.

Making regular physical contact is essential for maintaining closeness and intimacy in human relationships, be it romantic or familial. Haptic communication is very effective in conveying one's feelings and emotions as well as evoking a sense of presence in a remote

© Springer International Publishing AG 2017
A.D. Cheok et al. (Eds.): LSR 2016, LNAI 10237, pp. 115–127, 2017.
DOI: 10.1007/978-3-319-57738-8_11

environment [10]. In particular, kissing is one of the most natural and universal expressions of love and affection. In many cultures, kissing is also a common form of greeting and goodbye. Studies have shown that a higher frequency of romantic kissing between couples increases romantic satisfaction and reduces stress level [3]. Family members, especially parents and children, also kiss each other to express their love and care. Kissing is the most direct and effective way of sharing an intimate moment and internet communications should allow people to connect to each other through this form of interaction.

Kissenger is developed with the aim of enabling users to kiss each other remotely through a haptic interface that replicates real kissing sensations. This is an evolution of our previous work [19], which was a PC-controlled device. The latest development consists of a plugin device that connects to a mobile phone's audio jack and a mobile application that connects to the device and sends real-time data stream over the Internet. A usage scenario is shown in Fig. 1, a little girl from London kisses her grandmother in Tokyo remotely over the Internet through a mediating device while talking on their mobile phones as if they are in the same physical location. Accurate haptic stimulations are produced by the positional changes of an array of linear actuators in contact with the human lips. Bilateral force control is used such that both users feel the reflections of their own forces as well as the forces from each other. Force sensors are placed on top of the linear actuators to measure the output forces and provide feedback to the local force controllers.

Fig. 1. Concept of Kissenger. A little girl from London sends a kiss to her grandmother in Tokyo over the Internet

Finally, we will also explore ways to engage other sensory modalities such as digitally stimulating the senses of taste and smell [18] to provide a multisensory kissing experience.

2   Related Work

Researchers and the industry have been actively developing systems, frameworks and architectures for integrating haptics in various applications, e.g. augmented reality, teleoperation, task simulation. Universal haptic interfaces, such as Novint Falcon [15] and HapticMaster [22], offer some out-of-the-box options to implement haptic control systems without a tedious development cycle. However, these readily available systems are not made to be used with mobile phones, which pose several limitations on the form factor, bandwidth and computational resources. Haptic solutions for mobile devices are mostly restricted to vibrotactile stimulation rather than force feedback. It's necessary to design a portable task-specific system suitable for physical interactions (such as kissing) using mobile devices.

2.1 Kiss Communication

Previous works that explored the concept of telecommunicating kiss did not focus on transmitting the dynamics of forces. The Kiss Communicator by IDEO lab [2] is a concept prototype that records the breath pattern of the sender as he blows into it and plays back in the form of an animated light sequence. In [6], the moisture level on the kissing device is measured and transmitted to the receiver by varying the wetness of a motorized sponge to represent a kiss. The Kiss Transmission Device [20] from the Kaji-moto Laboratory is a real-time bilateral system that synchronizes the turning angle of a straw as the user swirls it around using his tongue.

2.2 Admittance and Impedance Controlled Systems

Differentiating the system structures of haptic devices is important at the outset of the design process. Two general classes of systems can be identified depending on the mechanical inputs and outputs of the haptic devices - admittance controlled systems and impedance controlled systems [8]. Admittance controlled systems measure force as inputs and generate motion outputs (position, velocity, acceleration) [7, 23]. They are often found in braille devices and haptic displays using actuator arrays. An example is Project FEELEX, which simulates haptic sensations and the texture of an object's surface using a linear actuator array [7]. In this system, the positions of the actuators are binary (up or down).

Impedance control systems are the reverse as they accept motion inputs and produce force outputs [4]. Both approaches could be implemented as open-loop or closed-loop if force or velocity sensors are used to provide feedback to the controllers.

2.3 Bilateral Control Methods

Designing a real-time bilateral force control to simulate the dynamic forces on the lips of the users is essential for a haptic interface capable of conveying a realistic kissing experience. Stability and transparency are two important factors used to measure the performance of a bilateral control system [9]. Stability depends on how well the controller counters time delay and package losses in the communication channel, which are major disturbances to the system. Transparency measures how closely the two devices (master and slave) follow the motions and positions of each other. In an ideal system with perfect transparency, the human operator should feel that they are directly touching the remote object without a mediating device [17]. Complete transparency cannot be achieved if the system is unstable. It is necessary for the controller to reduce the effects of time delay.

Many bilateral tele-manipulation systems are developed for humans to explore a remote environment or to interact with remote objects via a robotic manipulator [24, 25]. Human to human haptic communication over a network is investigated in some tele-handshake systems and they demonstrate different force and position control algorithms with disturbance compensation [12, 16, 21].

Solutions such as the scattering theory control by Anderson [1] and the wave variables control by Niemeyer [14]. Both approaches maintain stability by providing corrective actions to preserve passivity of the system. They convert time delay, which is modelled as a non-passive block, into a passive block to maintain passivity. The bilateral controller used in the remote handshake system described in [11] is based on scattering and wave variables control for stabilization and handling communication latency.

A drawback of the scattering approach or the wave variables control is that they deteriorate tracking performance. It is shown that using a local PID controller can attenuate this effect. When using a scattering matrix or wave filter for stabilization, A PID controller implemented at the slave side can improve the tracking performance of the system [26]. Using a PID controller alone on each side of the bilateral system also preserves the passivity of the system [5].

3   Design Considerations

Several factors are considered in designing the control system and hardware of the haptic communication device for mobile phones, including the mode of haptic stimulation, portability, communication delay, bandwidth and the stimulation of other sensory modalities such as smell.

Vibrotactile stimulation is commonly used as the mode of stimulation in many haptic systems as vibration motors are lightweight, cheap and easy to control. The vibration frequency and magnitude are varied to produce different textures and tactile sensations. However, the dynamics of the movements and pressure felt by the human lips during kissing cannot be accurately reproduced by vibrations alone. The mechanoreceptors on our lips respond to the changes in skin strain and deformation caused by external forces exerting on them. The haptic device needs to generate a series of localized forces in order to capture the haptic sensations during kissing. We designed an array of linear actuators positioned evenly across the lips to generate normal forces on the skin surface. The same number of force sensors resistors are placed on top of the actuators to measure the contact forces between the human user and the haptic interface. Although linear actuators with position encoders or embedded force sensors are commercially available, most products are too big for our application. Hence we use force sensor resistors in our system to provide force feedback.

In a field study conducted with the previous version of Kissenger, couples responded that it would be more convenient if they could use Kissenger while talking to their partners on the phone [19]. For a device designed for mobile phones, the challenge is to balance its functionalities with its size and weight in order to have a portable device. Small and lightweight components that consumes minimal power need to be chosen for the hardware. The study also mentions that some people feel embarrassed to kiss a machine in public as they are concerned that other people might find them weird. Thus the device should be designed in such a way that users feel comfortable using it in public. We believe that designing it as a plug-in gadget for mobile phones instead of a standalone device reduces the awkwardness of using it in public.

As discussed in the previous section, time delay present in the communication channel should be taken into consideration in designing the system control. Since mobile devices have lower memory and computational resources compared to computers, the data transmission speed between the haptic interface and mobile phones using audio jack is also relatively limited, the controller should accommodate a low sampling frequency with minimal memory usage and processing requirements.

Smell is another important aspect that directly affects our emotional responses to a kiss. It is well known that our sense of smell affects emotions more efficiently than any other sense. When two people are kissing, they are in close proximity enough to smell the body odor of each other. Experiments have shown that we are able to detect a class of genes present in body odor called the MHCs, which determines our sexual preference and compatibility to a person [23]. Hence, emitting the partner's body odor during kissing does not only create a stronger sense of physical presence but also strengthens our affection to that partner. Similarly, taste stimulations could also be integrated for a full multisensory kissing experience.

4 System Architecture

Considering the different aspects described in the previous section, we designed the Kissenger haptic interface as a small portable device that can easily plug into the audio jack of any mobile phone. Figure 2 shows a block diagram of the system architecture.

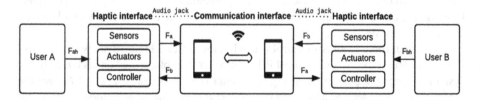

Fig. 2. System architecture of Kissenger consists of human users, a haptic interface with bilateral force control and a wireless Internet communication interface

4.1 System Control

During operation, a human user on each side of the system interacts with the haptic interface and exerts a varying force on the lip-like surface of the interface, represented by F_{ah} and F_{bh} in Fig. 2. The controller changes the positions of the linear actuators to reflect the forces transmitted from the partner and the user's own forces. The forces felt

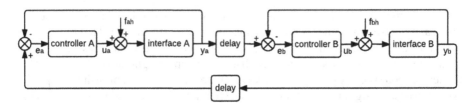

Fig. 3. Control block diagram for a bilateral force feedback haptic telecommunication system

by the user's lips are the contact forces (F_a and F_b in Fig. 2) between the lips and the haptic device measured by the force sensors on the surface of the device. In a perfectly transparent bilateral control system, the law of action and reaction must be realized hence the contact forces acting on both users should be equal at all times. In other words, the net force should be zero at all times. The positions of the actuators should also follow the positions of the partner user. Consider two users in the system, User A and User B, and factor in the communication time delay, the objectives of the controller can be expressed as follows:

$$F_a(t) - F_b(t - \tau) = 0, \; x_a(t) + x_b(t - \tau) = 0. \tag{1}$$

where F_a, F_b, are the contact forces between the user and the haptic device, x_a, x_b are the positions of the actuators relative to the origin for User and User B respectively. τ is the time delay of the communication channel.

The positions of the actuators are modelled as the lip surface of the remote human user and should reflect the forces of both users. The position of an actuator could simply relate to the net sum of the two contact forces by a proportional gain, as given by Eq. (2).

$$x_a(t) = K_s(F_a(t) - F_b(t - \tau)). \tag{2}$$

Different from other teleoperation systems with a master-slave configuration, in which human operators control a remote environment or object through a haptic interface, there are two active user inputs in this system and there is no distinction between a slave and a master.

A bilateral force feedback control is used in the system. Figure 3 shows the control block diagram of the system. A local PID controller is implemented on each side of the system to control the actuators using force data from both users. F_{ah} and F_{bh} are the forces exerted by users, u_a and u_b are the input commands to the actuators, y_a and y_b are the contact forces measured by the force sensors, and e_a and e_b are the errors between the force outputs from both sides. The system is closed-loop admittance controlled as it measures force as input and generate a positional output. Since the actuators do not have position encoders, the output forces are measured by force sensors and fed into the controller to close the control loop.

The output of the PID controller is denoted in Eq. (3). The system is discrete with a certain sampling frequency, as denoted by Eq. (4).

$$u_a(t) = K_p \left\{ e_a(t) + \frac{1}{T_i} \int_0^t e_a(\tau)d\tau + T_d \frac{de_a(t)}{dt} \right\}. \tag{3}$$

$$\xrightarrow{\Delta} K_p \left\{ e_a(\Delta t) + \frac{1}{T_i} \sum_{k=0}^t e_a(k\Delta t)\Delta t + T_d \frac{e_a(\Delta t)}{\Delta t} \right\}. \tag{4}$$

where

$$e_a = y_b - y_a, \quad e_b = y_a - y_b. \tag{5}$$

and K_p is the proportional gain, T_i is the integral time and T_d is the derivative time constant.

The constants are tuned depending on the linear properties of the force sensor derived from calibration, the stroke length of the linear actuator as well as the perceived stiffness of the haptic interface. Upper and lower limits of the actuator position are imposed to ensure safe operation.

4.2 Data Transmission

Force data is continuously transmitted between the two haptic interfaces via the Internet. As shown in Fig. 2, there are two stages in the data transmission channel - (1) audio signal transmission between the haptic interface and the mobile phone and (2) internet transmission between the two mobile phones.

Force sensor resistors are read by the microcontroller's analog inputs as 10-bit data. In order to maximize the speed and minimize error during data transmission, the data is compressed into 8 bits at the expense of resolution. Data is transmitted between the microcontroller and the mobile phone over audio signals using the Frequency Shift Keying (FSK) technique. The byte-sized force data is modulated to 4900 Hz for a low bit and 7350 Hz for a high bit and sent to the connected mobile phone through the microphone channel of the audio line.

The mobile phone demodulates the audio signal carrying the force data into digital bytes and sends it to the partner's phone over the Internet. When the other phone receives the force data, it processes the data and modulates it using the same FSK settings over an audio signal and sends to its haptic device through the left/right audio channel.

Latency occurs in both stages of the data transmission process. In the first stage (microcontroller to mobile phone), latency is consistent and controllable whereas in the second case (mobile phone to mobile phone) it depends on the quality of the internet connection of used by the devices. The total time delay is the measured as the time taken to send 1 byte from one haptic device to the other.

5 Implementation

We made a prototype of Kissenger for iOS devices (shown in Fig. 4), including the hardware of the haptic interface and an iOS mobile application.

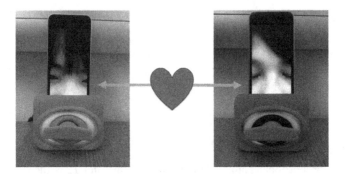

Fig. 4. Prototype of Kissenger. Users exchange kisses while having a video chat

The model of the haptic device is designed and made using a 3D printer with hard PLA material and soft rubber material. Arduino is used as the controller in the haptic device. RGB LEDs are used to provide users a visual feedback and to express emotions through colour. The colour of the LEDs changes according to the duration and intensity of the kiss.

5.1 Hardware

The haptic device consists of linear stepper motors, force sensor resistors and an Arduino microcontroller. The stroke, output force and power consumption of the actuators are some important parameters to consider when selecting linear actuators. There are several types of actuators that generate linear motion. Shape-memory alloy actuators produce weak forces and the output forces are difficult to control. Piezoelectric actuators normally have high driving voltages in the rage of 60 V–230 V, hence not suitable for battery operated devices. High precision miniature stepper motors are chosen for their size, power, output force/torque and controllability. A combination of lead screw and nut converts the rotary motion of a stepper motor into linear motion, making them into linear actuators. Precise positions changes can be controlled using microstepping.

Stepper motors consume the most power when stationary, hence they tend to run hot during standby. In order to avoid overheating, the motor drivers cut off the current to the motors after a period of inactivity.

Force sensor resistors (FSRs) are chosen to measure the output force for their flexibility, low cost, thinness and lightness. Although they are more prone to drift and are generally less accurate than load cells or strain gauges, the advantages of FSRs in size and power outweigh these drawbacks especially for a small size mobile device.

A 4-pin TRRS audio connector is used to connect the hardware device to iPhone. A FSK circuit is built and a FSK modem is implemented on both Arduino and iPhone for data transmission between the two devices. The baud rate of FSK transmission on Arduino obtained from empirical testing is about 100 bps.

5.2 Mobile Application

A mobile application is developed for iOS devices. Figure 5 shows two screenshots of the application.

Fig. 5. Screenshots of the Kissenger iOS app. Left: Users can choose a friend and start a video chat. Right: During the video chat, users can kiss each other using the device

It detects and connects to the hardware device when one is plugged in. Users can log in with Facebook, search and add their friends who are also using Kissenger. When a user starts a video chat with a friend, the application starts to send and receive data from the haptic device. Real-time force data is transmitted to the partner via the Internet using the Pubnub data streaming service. Users can also choose to change the LED colours of their partner's Kissenger device to convey different moods. A disadvantage of connecting to the audio jack of the phone is that headphones cannot be used during conversations.

6 User Scenarios

Kissenger can be used for both one-to-one communication and one-to-many communication where many Kissenger devices are connected to the same network.

Long distance lovers often communicate with their partners through video chats. With Kissenger, they can enhance this experience by kissing each other while looking at their faces and hearing their voices from the mobile phones. Parents can also use Kissenger to give their children a kiss on the cheek when they are away at work, as shown in Fig. 6.

Fig. 6. Usage scenario of Kissenger between a parent and a daughter

Apart from personal communications, Kissenger can also serve as a creative gadget for advertising or marketing celebrities. Pop idols can use Kissengers to interact with their fans by sending them a kiss on stage. Multiple Kissenger devices are connected to the same network and one device is selected to be the sender while others are receivers. Each receiver's device is actuated at the same time when the sender is sending a kiss.

7 Conclusion

We present a kiss communication interface for mobile phones that enables long distance families and friends to remotely kiss each other over the internet. This encourages physical interaction essential to maintain intimacy in long distance relationships.

7.1 Future Work

In the current prototype, the haptic device is attached to the bottom of a mobile phone which has limited space to embed the circuit, controller and multiple pairs of actuators, motor drivers and sensors. We redesigned the model as a mobile phone case (shown in Fig. 7) to make more space at the back of the phone so that it can accommodate more sensors and actuators. With the added space for hardware, the device still keeps its portability with improved aesthetics and functionality since many people use mobile phone cases as protection or decoration.

Fig. 7. 3D models of the Kissenger haptic interface in the form of a mobile phone case with additional actuators and sensors

The 3D design in Fig. 7 shows the latest model is capable of housing 6 pairs of actuators and sensors, 3 for each lower lip and upper lip. We believe that this new design would generate a more realistic kissing sensation. A more flexible and softer material close to the human skin will be used for the lip part.

Currently the system only implements a single degree of freedom force control. We will explore multiple degrees of freedom and implement more realistic kissing dynamics such as tongue movements. A fuzzy logic PD controller [13] will be experimented considering the different modes of operation, such as when one side is not in contact with the user or in free motion.

We will also investigate ways to incorporate the scent communication device, Scentee, to emit the perfume or a distinctive scent associated with the user's partner to create a multisensory experience. Lastly, other factors such as temperature and moisture will also be considered in our design.

Acknowledgements. This work is supported by the Osaka University Scholarship for Overseas Research Activities 2014.

References

1. Anderson, R.J., Spong, M.W.: Bilateral control of teleoperators with time delay. IEEE Trans. Autom. Control **34**(5), 494–501 (1989)
2. Buchenau, M., Suri, J.F.: Experience prototyping. In: Proceedings of the 3rd Conference on Designing Interactive Systems: Processes, Practices, Methods, and Techniques, pp. 424–433. ACM (2000)
3. Floyd, K., Boren, J.P., Hannawa, A.F., Hesse, C., McEwan, B., Veksler, A.E.: Kissing in marital and cohabiting relationships: effects on blood lipids, stress, and relationship satisfaction. W. J. Commun. **73**(2), 113–133 (2009)
4. Force Dimension: Force Dimension delta.6 (2015). http://www.forcedimension.com/products/delta-6/overview. Accessed 16 Aug 2015
5. Forouzantabar, A., Talebi, H.A., Sedigh, A.K.: Bilateral control of master–slave manipulators with constant time delay. ISA Trans. **51**(1), 74–80 (2012)
6. Hemmert, F., Gollner, U., Löwe, M., Wohlauf, A., Joost, G.: Intimate mobiles: grasping, kissing and whispering as a means of telecommunication in mobile phones. In: Proceedings of the 13th International Conference on Human Computer Interaction with Mobile Devices and Services, pp. 21–24. ACM (2011)
7. Iwata, H., Yano, H., Nakaizumi, F., Kawamura, R.: Project FEELEX: adding haptic surface to graphics. In: Proceedings of the 28th Annual Conference on Computer Graphics and Interactive Techniques, pp. 469–476. ACM (2001)
8. Kern, T.A.: General System Structures. In: Hatzfeld, C., Kern, T.A. (eds.) Engineering Haptic Devices: A Beginner's Guide for Engineers, 2nd edn, pp. 169–179. Springer, London (2014)
9. Lawrence, D., Others: Stability and transparency in bilateral teleoperation. IEEE Trans. Robot. Autom. **9**(5), 624–637 (1993)
10. Minato, T., Nishio, S., Ishiguro, H.: Evoking an affection for communication partner by a robotic communication medium. In: Proceedings of the 8th ACM/IEEE International Conference on Human-Robot Interaction Demo Session, vol. 7 (2013)
11. Miyoshi, T., Terasima, K., Buss, M.: A design method of wave filter for stabilizing non-passive operating system. In: Computer Aided Control System Design, 2006 IEEE International Conference on Control Applications, 2006 IEEE International Symposium on Intelligent Control, pp. 1318–1324. IEEE (2006)
12. Miyoshi, T., Ueno, Y., Kawase, K., Matsuda, Y., Ogawa, Y., Takemori, K., Terashima, K.: Development of handshake gadget and exhibition in Niconico Chokaigi. In: Kajimoto, H., Ando, H., Kyung, K.-U. (eds.) Haptic Interaction. Lecture Notes in Electrical Engineering, pp. 267–272. Springer, Japan (2015)
13. Ni, L., Wang, D.W.L.: A human-to-human force-reflecting teleoperation system using fuzzy logic controller tuning. J. Intell. Robot. Syst. **48**(2), 209–224 (2007)
14. Niemeyer, G., Slotine, J.-J.E.: Stable adaptive teleoperation. IEEE J. Oceanic Eng. **16**(1), 152–162 (1991)
15. Novint Technologies Inc.: Novint Falcon (2012). http://www.novint.com/index.php/products/novintfalcon. Accessed 16 Aug 2015
16. Park, S., Park, S., Baek, S.-Y., Ryu, J.: A human-like bilateral tele-handshake system: preliminary development. In: Auvray, M., Duriez, C. (eds.) EUROHAPTICS 2014. LNCS, vol. 8619, pp. 184–190. Springer, Heidelberg (2014). doi:10.1007/978-3-662-44196-1_23

17. Jagannath Raju, G., Verghese, G.C., Sheridan, T.B.: Design issues in 2-port network models of bilateral remote manipulation. In: Proceedings of IEEE International Conference on Robotics and Automation,pp. 1316–1321. IEEE (1989)
18. Ranasinghe, N., Karunanayaka, K., Cheok, A.D., Fernando, O.N.N., Nii, H., Gopalakrishnakone, P.: Digital taste and smell communication. In: Proceedings of the 6th International Conference on Body Area Networks, pp. 78–84. ICST (Institute for Computer Sciences, Social-Informatics and Telecommunications Engineering) (2011)
19. Saadatian, E., Samani, H., Parsani, R., Pandey, A.V., Li, J., Tejada, L., Cheok, A.D., Nakatsu, R.: Mediating intimacy in long-distance relationships using kiss messaging. Int. J. Hum.-Comput. Stud. **72**(10), 736–746 (2014)
20. Takahashi, N., Kuniyasu, Y., Sato, M., Fukushima, S., Furukawa, M., Hashimoto, Y., Kajimoto, H.: A remote haptic communication device that evokes a feeling of kiss. Interaction 2 (2011)
21. Tsunashima, N., Katsura, S.: Bilateral control based on human model for haptic communication. In: 2010 11th IEEE International Workshop on Advanced Motion Control, pp. 319–324. IEEE (2010)
22. Van der Linde, R.Q., Lammertse, P., Frederiksen, E., Ruiter, B.: The HapticMaster, a new high-performance haptic interface. In: Proceedings of Eurohaptics, pp. 1–5 (2002)
23. Wedekind, C., Penn, D.: MHC genes, body odours, and odour preferences. Nephrol. Dial. Transp. **15**(9), 1269–1271 (2000)
24. Winkler, A., Suchy, J.: Possibilities of Force Based Interaction with Robot Manipulators. INTECH Open Access Publisher (2007)
25. Yamanouchi, W., Yokokura, Y., Katsura, S., Ohishi, K.: Bilateral teleoperation with dimensional scaling for realization of mobile-hapto. In: 34th Annual Conference of IEEE Industrial Electronics, IECON 2008, pp. 1590–1595. IEEE (2008)
26. Yoshino, T., Kawai, Y.: Improving tracking performance in teleoperation of haptic mouse using wave filter. In: Proceedings of 3rd International Symposium on Technology for Sustainability (ISTS2013), pp. 79–80 (2013)

Sex with Robots for Love Free Encounters

Lynne Hall[(✉)]

University of Sunderland, Sunderland, UK
lynne.hall@sunderland.ac.uk

Abstract. This paper considers sex with robots for love free encounters within the context of pornographic experiences. Leisure sex and pornography are briefly outlined, along with the potential of the market. Limited research on both the user experience of pornography and the physical functionality of sex robots is highlighted. The physical embodiment of sex robots is considered, questioning whether we need human-like robots or something else entirely. Technological advances for pornography and their relevance for sex robots are explored examining the potential offered through the integration of Virtual Reality, teledildonics, soft and wearable robots. The potential of categorising sex robots as fantasy hardware is considered seeking to provide a palatable terminology. This paper concludes that researchers need to engage with the Porn Sector in creating innovative sexual experiences with robots, aiming to create a new type of sexual experience, rather than replicating humans as seen in most science fiction.

Keywords: Sex robots · Pornography · Teledildonics · Soft robots · Human robot interaction · User experience

1 Introduction

Socially we are often encouraged to entwine sex and love, yet there are multiple views, perspectives and experiences of sex, a limited number of which incorporate or relate to love and vice versa. This paper discusses the potential of robots for sexual activity that whilst it can be used to enhance a loving relationship most frequently is not. Instead, pornography is representative of a sexual activity that is quintessentially not related to love.

There are supporters for the perspective that one day we will create robots that we can love and even marry. Yet, it must be queried how sensible, natural or wise it is to love a created object, even one that has the 'look and feel' of a living being. Whilst a robot may simulate life, fundamentally it is not living. It cares not one jot about anything but adequately completing the code stored in its technology. Yes, it may be possible to create robots that are simulacrums of reality, however, this is all they are and thus the idea of evoking emotions such as love through human-robot interaction seems oddly inappropriate.

Of course there is the argument that some people need to feel loved and that a robot could provide an ideal solution for someone who isn't being loved. I'm not convinced, for whilst another living being may require love, a created object, even one that appears to love in return does not really require or reciprocate this love. Requiring a suspension

© Springer International Publishing AG 2017
A.D. Cheok et al. (Eds.): LSR 2016, LNAI 10237, pp. 128–136, 2017.
DOI: 10.1007/978-3-319-57738-8_12

of disbelief to enable durable love seems unrealistic and ultimately you know your lover was created by a bunch of computer scientists and engineers. Irrespective of such doubts, the popular vision that we will co-exist with lifelike humanoid robots for companionship, love and sex continues to dominate. This vision is strongly influenced by science fiction, with a whole host of lifelike robots, played by people, to choose from. To make the fictional narrative interesting and effective, the robots whether sex workers or loving partner, exhibit emotional and social traits of 'real humans.'

In responding to this fictional vision of the social, emotional humanoid robot, the Human Robot Interaction research community has largely focused on steps towards creating loving, caring robots that are able to socially interact, with significant literature on affect and emotions in social robotics. The focus has been on the robot 'mind' and particularly the affective component, often with long term relationships as the context. However, do robots really need to be affective to provide a sexual experience for the user? With humans, even the most casual single liaison inevitably involves some social interaction, so intuitively the answer would be yes, sex robots should have some social capability. However, whilst affect has a role, surely more importantly the sex robot should be able to autonomously exhibit and physically respond to/for sexual pleasure.

The technical challenges surrounding physical embodiment for sex robots are immense, yet there has been relatively little focus on creating physical embodiments of sex robots. Physically embodied robots such as Nao, Pepper and Baxter have no sexual capacity. Although Pepper's purchasers were required to confirm that they would not use Pepper sexually, it is challenging to imagine how Pepper could be used as it is just a plastic doll with no sexual characteristics or orifices with only simple manipulation potential.

If we consider creating a robot for an excellent sexual experience for the user, then the user requirements are significantly reduced if our focus is on physical, sexual arousal and pleasure within a context that does not require love. Removing, love, social and emotional relationships from the requirements for the sex robot is commonly depicted in futuristic settings by sex robots operating as sex workers. However, perhaps the future for sex with robots might be something completely different from that portrayed in the media. Instead, could sex robots, like other hardware - such as consoles, form a part of our leisure activities. This paper explores the potential for sex robots to enhance a typical individual leisure experience, that of the user experience of pornography.

2 Leisure Sex and Pornography

A 'vanilla' view of sex still continues to dominate popular culture, particularly in the media, with healthy, appropriate sex often seen as an activity between consenting, loving, often heterosexual adults typically in a long-term relationship. Complementary to this, Attwood and Smith's discussion of leisure sex highlights a myriad of sexual practices and perspectives within "*a modern, mediatized sexual culture whose symbolic resources valorize revelation and hedonism rather than discretion and self-discipline*" [1].

Leisure sex is on the increase and gaining acceptance, for example, we are no longer shocked by the casual hook-ups of celebrities, merely titillated and amused. Casual hook- ups, affairs and sex as fun are becoming a more socially acceptable activity. This trend has clearly been facilitated by technology, with significant growth in hook-up and 'cheating' sites; social networks to share and gain experiences; increasing availability of adult content, such as on-line strip shows, sex web-cams, along with a significant amount industry and user generated pornographic content; and growing use of adult interactive virtual reality platforms across a range of consoles and devices.

Whilst much on-line leisure sex has focused on facilitating sexual activity between people, there is a growth in providing on-line sexual experiences that do not require another person. There are obvious benefits to this if the sex provides the required arousal and experience whilst avoiding potential dangers of intimate engagement, such as disease or unpleasant encounters, and of course some of the social consequences of getting 'caught.' On-line sexual experiences that do not involve another person are often pornographic, with content ranging from non-interactive video, audio and photos of real people to interactions with digital sex partners with no human in the loop.

There are many who argue that sex and pornography are, and should be, different things [2]. However, this would naively assume that the distinction between pornography and sex relates to the mechanics of how one physically engages in sexual activity. Instead the distinction is actually made to facilitate a vision of pornography as something morally deviant, harmful and unnatural as compared to a married couple having loving sex [3].

Pornography is part of many people's sexual arousal and activities, sitting on the spectrum of everyday, typical sexual experiences One of the most widely cited set of porn statistics [4] identified that every second 28,258 internet users are viewing porn; 25% of all search engine requests are pornography related; and 35% of all internet downloads are pornographic. These statistics are not without problems or critique [5, 6], but they have achieved status from their frequent repetition and resonate with the common sense belief that porn is an ever-increasing and regular on-line activity for many people.

Whilst there is some use of pornography by couples, predominantly we watch porn alone. And the emphasis is on watching rather than interaction. With this focus on the individual and non-interactive user experience, where pornography does differ from sex is in its inability to provide a sense of sexual intimacy, something that is inevitably generated through a sexual encounter between participants, however brief.

With the advent of sex robots, pornography could be extended through robotics into a sexual act performed on an individual by another entity. Thus intimacy of sorts, albeit not with another person, begins to be possible in an individual context. This sexual intimacy may be very different to that which we experience with people. However, how we use pornography is also different to how we experience sex with others.

3   Any Guidelines for the Sex Robot for Pornography?

The significant size of the porn industry and widespread reporting of frequent use, would suggest that on-line porn use would be a well-studied domain, with plentiful design, development, interaction and evaluation advice for the user experience that could be used to ground Porn Robots. Unfortunately, this is not the case, with [7] noting that "the intense proliferation of and access to pornography occasioned by the Internet is one of its most important and least studied effects." There is a recognised need to consider sexuality and human computer (sexual) interaction [8, 9] argues that "HCI has a unique contribution to make to the broader study of pornography." This hasn't happened, and as noted in [8]'s comprehensive review of HCI and sexuality: "Works on sexual technology such as pornography, sex toys and health equipment are very few in number."

Work on sex robots is largely speculative and about attitudes to what might be and what we might need to think about. Much of this focuses on personal, social and cultural impact which largely relies on sex robots becoming pseudo-people, just as in science-fiction (e.g. Humans, Westworld). Thus, although there are studies relating to how relationships may be with sex robots, what the ethics might be, how we might live with them, love them, decide to buy them, etc. what is lacking is the sex robot itself.

Academic speculation has sparked media interest, culminating in articles implying that sex robots will be purchasable in the very near future. More, that these sex robots will provide intimacy, and be able to converse and interact like another being. This has resulted in user expectations of sex robots being impossibly high.

Currently, there are no sex robots, with the frequently referenced Roxxxy yet to be seen and reviewed by the scientific community and viewed by Levy as a hoax. And whilst there is a nod to technical challenge in the academic literature on robot sex, the focus has been on thought and potential, the 'what if' scenarios, rather than actually making the robots and evaluating what can be achieved.

Whilst the research community remains nervously on the sidelines and fails to engage with the design, development and evaluation of technology for pornography, the Porn Industry has no such qualms. As with earlier technologies including photography, cinema, user-generated content [10], software affiliation and Tube sites [11], the Porn Industry is clearly willing to invest and use any technology they can to progress their sector. And robots are within their sights.

4   Requirements for the Sex Robot - Technological Responses to Pornographic Challenges

Whilst pornography is often considered and advertised as 'leaving nothing to the imagination' and 'providing an immersive experience,' currently these claims are only partially met. With pornography restricted to visual and auditory stimuli, there is clearly a need for the imagination to fill the gaps left by the other senses to increase the sense of immersion. And until recently, on-line porn was screen based in a non-immersive media format that is clearly physically separate from the user. Times are changing, with VR technologies, particularly the emergence of VR headsets such as Oculus Rift, Samsung Gear and Google Cardboard offering pornography a way to provide full audio and visual immersion.

The inconvenience of wearing a VR headset is massively outweighed by the benefits of the increased appeal of VR Porn, with sales in VR headsets revealing clear consumer interest. Notably, Oculus has placed almost no restrictions on content to be developed for the Oculus Rift. This effectively opens the way for pornographers, such as SugarDVD 'the Netflix of Porn,' who are developing VR content [12] along with a dedicated VR Porn channel. Predictions of trends by companies such as Market Watch are that the Adult Content area of VR will have similar sales potential as the game sector.

With VR, it is technologically possible to convince ourselves that we are in an audio-visual reality, thus hearing and sight, the two key foci of porn videos can already become a realistic experience. This move to VR for pornography highlights an important alternative when considering sex with robots, with the opportunity to provide the robot's audio and visual aesthetic through a headset rather than within the physical embodiment of the robot itself.

Our goal with sex robots for pornography is to facilitate the user in individual sexual activity within the context of the pornographic narrative. With appearance, sound and to some degree sense of presence in the narrative dealt with by VR, then our focus turns to embodiment. Whilst VR removes an immense number of technical challenges for sex robot developers, in some ways it is removing the easiest challenge of all which is the simplest physical representation of the sex partner, that is another human.

If a sex robot needs to have a humanlike embodiment, then there are already potential options under development. Abyss Creations have had considerable success with Real-Doll, a high-end product at $12 k or more. RealDolls are realistic lifelike products, except that the dolls are static, inanimate objects, devoid of life. RealDoll dolls are posable - but still and quiet. Incorporating robotics into such dolls is possible. Where humanoid robots are created, such as by Ishiguro's lab, the results may provide lifelike behaviour, but the insides are full of hard electronics without sexual functionality.

RealDoll have been investing heavily in AI and doll robotics [13]. Like many contemplating love and sex with robots their focus is not just on the physical, but also on improving the dolls ability to socially interact including verbally and to exhibit and respond to affect. There are rumours that Abyss Creations will release a RealDoll that is a sex robot in 2017, however, with the mechanical challenges significant, the goal of achieving a sensual, quasi-realistic sexual experience with lifelike humans resolving hardware issues from noise to texture to heat still seems unlikely in the near future.

With dolls not affordable and VR able to mitigate the challenge of auditory and visual embodiment, then should this change what the physical embodiment of the sex robot could be? Do we need a whole body or even a body at all? If our requirements are for the robot to facilitate sexual activity, should we focus on sexual stimuli and thus the sexual embodiment of the robot, focusing on SexTech's potential to morph into the basis of a sex robot.

Sex toys and particularly teledildonics offer considerable potential for the sex robot. Although they have been primarily aimed at long distance lovers, with a human representing their embodiment through the teledildonic such devices are equally relevant for interactive virtual sex with a character. There has been some use of them in sex games, such as those by SOM with linked teledildonics using sensors to provide relevant feedback to the application. TENGA have gone further providing linked VR via headset and teledildonics offering an interactive, immersive experience. And with a much stronger pornographic feel is Pornhub's Twerking Butt, which includes a VR headset and sex toy with a range of options and narratives.

5 Reconsidering the Appearance of the Sex Robot

A key element of sexual pleasure for many relates to the visual experience. We currently naturally see sexual activity in terms of one another and our physical makeup and design. However, just as the perfect robotic paint sprayer looks little like us in its most effective implementation, why would we expect the robotic sexual partner to look like us? Do we really need aesthetically pleasing robots that look like attractive sex partners? And even if we don't, would we want to have sex with something that looked operational and factory spec? Very few teledildonics are attractive, they typically look like crude, sex toys with a clear functional goal. However, this is no longer an issue, no need to keep our eyes tight closed and work hard on the imagination and fantasy... instead we just gaze into the Oculus Rift with an engaging pornographic narrative providing a new user experience of sex.

If we look at robots used in domestic situations, we can see that our views of robot appearance tailored by sci-fi TV, books and films are delightfully absurd. The robot that actually hoovers the house has little visual resemblance to a maid, yet they do the job well. And so, if a well-designed robot could do the sexual job well, why are we waiting for Jude Law as the AI Gigolo? And if it is him we are waiting for, can't that just be via a VR feed? By removing the need for the robot to look lifelike by providing it via alternative technology such as via a VR headset we completely free up the requirements for the physical embodiment of the robot.

Whilst there is much interest in interactive virtual sex, such experiences typically require the participants to be real rather than robots. Where characters replace avatars the approach tends to be relatively simplistic, with user input often limited to story world selection, partner (character) appearance with a limited number of alternate endings. To achieve good robot pornography requires increased sensory input for the user and autonomous sexual reciprocity from the robot rather than simplistic teledildonics tied to a script providing more or less the same experience to all users.

There have been significant advances in physical computing, with increasingly sensitive sensors and actuators. With the current trend in the sex toy market to gather user data, the understanding and application of effective sexual mechanics will increase. Whilst there is concern about this data use, most users are content for their data to be used to improve the next model.

For the sex robot, data will be key, initially in establishing parameters, actions and behaviours with their various physical embodiments. Then, as interaction history develops, the robot will need to respond in line with the user's requirements and expectations. In some ways, this will be similar to training a speech recogniser. With this adaptation, the sex robot will provide a personalized sexual experience of the pornographic narrative based on the user's preferences.

And this will be key for the sex robot used in pornography, with many porn users watching a wide variety of pornography across a range of genres. This variety is a significant issue for the sex robot, as most users will want to be able to engage in multiple experiences using the same technological set-up. Just as with games consoles users will want to interact with a range of narratives and a variety of characters through the single robot. Thus, if the requirement changes from the perfect single sex partner to something that can be many sex partners, then the issue is can the robot morph physically representing multiple lovers rather than does the robot look like a particular individual.

Fundamentally a robot is a physically embodied entity with some degree of autonomy in behaviour and interaction. Further, and of particular importance for sexual activity, that this embodiment must enable physical, sexual activity and this physicality must include more than visual and auditory stimuli. Whilst for sex robots this can result in quasi-human designs, for example in the form of sensor filled dolls that could synch with and act out virtual character's moves whilst providing haptic feedback, there are alternatives. As we move away from the sex robot companion ideal towards the requirements for an interactive experience of pornography provided by an ensemble of sexually arousing narrative, VR, SexTech and robots, we must resist our functional fixedness to the human body as the provider of sexual experience.

Recent developments in soft robotics [14] could mean that rather than our traditional AI gigolo what we actually need is a wearable robot moulded intimately to ourselves. For engaging in sexual activity wearable robots offer an interesting avenue, with soft robotics having potential to enhance haptics and teledildonics. Thus, why not design a sex robot as a wearable, soft robot, able to morph and change as required, in line with the user's needs and requirements and the pornographic narrative. Coupled with an immersive VR experience solving the visual and auditory challenges, particularly removing the issue of the aesthetic of the robot this integration offers considerable potential for providing a novel porn experience, one that could include significant interactivity.

Whilst soft and wearable robots are still at a relatively early stage and developed primarily within the health and defence sectors, they do offer real potential as a device for pornographic interactivity. Wearing a soft robot, packed full of biosensors and technology could enable the robot to provide intimate pleasure tailored both to the narrative in the watched pornography and to the responses of the user. This symbiosis of soft robot and human would allow the robot to focus its autonomous intentions and behaviours to meeting the user's non-visual and non-audio sexual pleasure requirements and expectations, offering touch and feel sensations.

This is challenging for a robot as it will need to support a wide range of pornographic experiences rather than just one. This may be possible with wearable soft robots, however, intuitively it can be suggested additional haptic interfaces will be needed to enable users to experience shape and texture.

6 Sweetening the Concept

By integrating sex with robots and pornography, creating robot porn, we need to consider the terminology and its potential impact. With the negative connotations and strong antiporn lobby are we doing robots a disservice by tagging them with porn?

Instead, could we suggest we are actually creating robots to support masturbation and personal sexual gratification? Although masturbation has received its share of bad press, there is general acceptance that it is not intrinsically harmful, whilst porn is still often viewed as deviant. However, it is still something that is distasteful for many, with limited social discussion.

Or instead, could we say that as an important element of pornography is fantasy [15], that we are providing fantasy sex robots. This is so much more pleasant as a term than porn robots and clearly distinguishes these robots, which are intended for love free encounters, from robots developed for other types of sex. This sanitization to sexual experience enhanced through technology rather than some strange kink such as robot-porn may even enable us more easily to talk about our experiences... "I did that new fantasy XXX the other night."

Undoubtedly robot porn will gain its own terminology, with the press already high-lighting the likely dangers of this approach. The Porn Industry don't give a damn, their eyes are on the money and this is clearly a massively lucrative area. And more, this investment from the porn sector will impact significantly on almost any other interactive experience. The technologies developed to improve the porn experience will have valuable applications in sectors such as games and interactive movies.

7 Discussion

SugarDVD claim that they are "pioneering the future of what sex looks like." So, what should we do? Should we engage or should we hold back and let the porn sector decide what users will want. The merger of pornography and human-robot interaction should provide a tailored experience through multiple possible narrative contexts meeting the user's sexual expectations in terms of pace, skills and experiences. This combination of robotics, pornography, soft robots, teledildonics, sensors and other technologies would provide a new form of sexual experience. Engaging with pornographic media would be extended from an audio-visual watching experience to an immersive engagement with completely realistic audio visual quality, tactile and sensory stimulation, responsive interactivity and a very enjoyable new form of leisure sex.

This new outlet for leisure sex has no relevance to love and human relationships but instead provides the user with a novel sexual experience. There will always be those who raise issues such as technology addiction, but would this fantasy sex robot be addictive? If the robot was social and emotional then yes this could be really addictive, but if it just offered you good sex? Perhaps to some, but these will be few, although there has always been plentiful moral outrage about the impacts of porn [16]. Would this wearable soft robot give you unrealistic expectations of what to expect in sexual encounters. Possibly, but for most of us, no.

With pornography having primarily negative connotations, unsurprisingly robotics has largely remained shy of this area with a lack of research focus on creating robots that could enhance the pornographic experience. Although pornography is often viewed through a negative lens in robotics we should avoid such a response and instead perceive of pornography neutrally and as a way of obtaining investment to develop technology that will significantly change the user experience both for pornography and interactions in many other domains.

8 Conclusion

The use of robots for pornography is inevitable and underway, thus it would be eminently sensible for robotics to engage with an established, durable and growing sector with finance available for creating porn robots. Whilst there will still be a market for high end life like sex robots, this paper proposes an alternative, moving away from the robot's appearance to the sexual experience. By integrating soft and wearable robots, VR headsets, haptics and teledildonics in a pornographic narrative, a new experience can be provided targeting sexual pleasure requirements across a range of senses other than audio and visual. Such developments will have significant value and application beyond the porn sector with clear relevance to domains such as video games, virtual worlds and interactive movies.

References

1. Attwood, F., Smith, C.: Leisure sex: more sex! Better sex! Sex is fucking brilliant! Sex, Sex, Sex, SEX. In: Blackshaw, T. (ed.) Routledge Handbook of Leisure Studies, pp. 325–336 (2015)
2. Boyle, K.: Everyday Pornographies. Routledge, London (2010)
3. Smith, C., Attwood, F.: Anti/pro/critical porn studies. Porn Stud. 1, 7–23 (2014)
4. OnlineMBA: The Stats on Internet Pornography. Online MBA (2010). http://www.onlinemba.com/blog/the-stats-on-internet-porn/
5. Ruvolo, J.: How Much of the Internet is Actually for Porn. Forbes (2011). http://www.forbes.com/sites/julieruvolo/2011/09/07/how-much-of-the-internet-is-actually-for-porn/. Accessed 23 May 2013
6. Richardson, N., Smith, C., Werndly, A.: Studying Sexualities: Theories, Representations and Cultures, p. 155. Palgrave Macmillan, London (2013)
7. Keilty, P.: Embodiment and desire in browsing online pornography. In: 2012 iConference (iConference 2012), pp. 41–47 (2012)
8. Kannabiran, G., Bardzell, J., Bardzell, S.: How HCI talks about sexuality: discursive strategies, blind spots, and opportunities for future research. In: CHI 2011 (2011)
9. Silverberg, C.: Problematizing porn: ideas on sexuality, intimacy and the place of pornography in HCI research. In: Sexual Interactions: Why We Should Talk About Sex in HCI (Workshop at CHI 2006) (2006)
10. Lehman, P.: You and Voyeurweb: illustrating the shifting representation of the penis on the internet with user-generated content. Cinema J. 46(4), 108–116 (2007)
11. Wallace, B.: The Geek-Kings of Smut, New York (2011)
12. Grubb, J.: Strap on Your Oculus Rift And Get Ready: Interactive Porn is Coming. VentureBeat (2014). http://venturebeat.com/2014/05/21/strap-on-your-oculus-rift-and-get-ready-interactive-porn-is-coming/. Accessed 04 Sep 2015
13. Gurley, G.: Is This the Dawn of the Sexbots? (NSFW). Vanity Fair, May 2015
14. Rus, D., Tolley, M.T.: Design, fabrication and control of soft robots. Nature 521(7553), 467–475 (2015)
15. Barker, M.: The 'problem' of sexual fantasies. Porn Stud. 1, 143–160 (2014)
16. McNair, B.: Rethinking the effects paradigm in porn studies. Porn Stud. 1, 161–171 (2014)

Robots and Intimacies: A Preliminary Study of Perceptions, and Intimacies with Robots

Chamari Edirisinghe[1,2(✉)] and Adrian David Cheok[1,2]

[1] Imagineering Institute, IDM Lab Sdn Bhd, Anchor 5, Mall of Medini,
4, Lebuh Medini Utara, 79200 Nusajaya, Johor, Malaysia
{chamari,adrian}@imagineeringinstitute.org
[2] City, University of London, Northampton Square, London, EC1V 0HB, UK

Abstract. When David Levy first introduced the subject of 'love and sex with robots', he became a provocateur of a conversation that spread from morality to the rights of robots. With the rapid development in Artificial Intelligence, love and sex with robots is expected to be a reality in near future. However, the question remains, how much humans understand and accept intimacies with robots. We argue that perceptions of human-robot interactions (HRI) have a certain impact on how individuals comprehend intimacies with robots. In this study, a pilot study of first stage of a series of studies, we examined the perception of robots, and intimacies with robots, and realized our sample created a 'self and other', and 'over there, but not here' distinction when it comes to the perception of HRI. This stance, we like to identify as an adoption of a moral position, not simply with regards to love and sex with robots, but also communicating to HRI.

Keywords: Robots · Intimacies · Human-robot interactions · Perceptions · Love

1 Introduction

1.1 Background

Connections, relationships, and intimacies between humans and robots have been part of the fantasy of science fiction. Now, it is a conversation in real life, opening possibilities to experience a future, hitherto a mere fiction. Although, robots are highly advanced and largely negatively represented in fiction, real life robots have been part of the human every day for some time now. Robots play a significant, yet not visible roles as efficient machines programed to replace humans in doing tedious repetitive tasks. Service robots are developed to play the roles of domestic staff, to vacuum the floor, or mow the lawn. Then, there are personal robots who performed the tasks of personal concierges, robot toys, and robot arms etc. In all these roles, robots serve and perform a designated task to automated abilities. In other words, robots are advanced tools, accepting certain instructions, and performing assignments.

© Springer International Publishing AG 2017
A.D. Cheok et al. (Eds.): LSR 2016, LNAI 10237, pp. 137–147, 2017.
DOI: 10.1007/978-3-319-57738-8_13

The process, or let us call it[1] as the connection, is proceeding from human to robots; requests, instruction, and commands from humans to be adhere to and execute by robots. This pattern of connection is challenged through the developments in artificial intelligence (AI) where, rather than listening to instructions and acting upon it, robots initiate conversation, such as among humans. In other words, robots with cognitive abilities, who comprehend, reason, and preform. The meaningful human-robot interactions have the possibility to develop a human-robot relationship, based on not commands and actions, but on emotional bonds, because both parties are sharing and experiencing emotions.

Levy [1] asks "...if a robot behaves as though it has feelings, can we reasonably argue that it does not?...". This contested the next level of HRI, where complexities of human emotions are pitted against emotions of robots for an authenticity. In the movie 'Bicentennial Man', the robot falls in love with a human and vice versa, however, is the love robot feel for the human any less poignant than human love for the robot? While Levy [1] argues that one can believe robots having feelings if there is a behavior pattern to back them, there is the argument that humans programed the robot, giving it a cognitive platform, thus controlling the feelings and behavior patterns. The 'Bicentennial Man' is a robot independent in cognition, making moral judgments per situations. At this juncture, we arrive at the point where science fiction has been wondering (and frightening), if robots are given the ability to develop their own cognition, to reason and feel, would their moral judgments give them power over humans? More than half a century ago, Asimov[2] [2] answered this matter by imposing rules for robots, which will certainly defeat the purpose of HRI. However, it brings the question of morality associated with thoughts and behaviors, to which Coeckelberg [3] writes an interesting essay. What if a robot could make a moral judgement with the cognitive capacity given to it, and feel and behave accordingly, and if it communicates feelings of love and express the desire for physical intimacies, would we feel threatened, and respond accordingly? When robots are evolved to accommodate, and reciprocate human emotions, humans will find it unimaginable to live without them, bringing forth the rationality to Levy's argument.

Human-robot relationship is not about to happen overnight, since most of the possibilities in discussion here are hypothesizes. But the discussions are happening, because hypothesizing robotic future is not strange to us. Acceptance of robots as companions and lovers first required the acceptance of robots in general as more than assistive labor, toys, and an unknown threat. A very recent study on the layperson's view of robots concluded that the perception of robots are still as mechanical bodies [4] and another

---

[1] 1999 movie Directed by Chris Columbus and Co-produce by Touchstone Pictures & Columbia Pictures.

[2] (1) A robot may not injure a human being or, through inaction, allow a human being to come to harm. (2) A robot must obey orders given it by human beings except where such orders would conflict with the First Law. (3) A robot must protect its own existence as long as such protection does not conflict with the First or Second Law.
Later he added a forth law or zeroth law 'A robot may not harm humanity, or, by inaction, allow humanity to come to harm'.

study has examined the 'Othering' in human-robot interactions [5], presenting us with layers of challenges in perception in HRI.

As Scheutlz and Arnold [6] discussed in their paper, the human acceptance of sex robots falls within the existing connections and relationships. Human-robot interactions, at this point in time, are rather feudal in structure, robots being programed to take instructions, obey, and execute, just as peasants were conditioned to accept the establishment in feudal societies. With time, robots will be programed to comprehend humans, converse, and build relationship through mutual understandings. Robots will evolve to be emotionally and cognitively intelligent and to communicate and reciprocate thoughts and feelings. With time, Human-robot relationship will not be that of a sex robot and human, but a fully emotional and physical bonding, a sharing and caring union of mutual understanding. It is understandably important for bonds between humans and robots be bidirectional, and if a robot can have the capacity to learn, reason and evolve, it will contribute to the relationship to satisfy its requirements, as well as mindful of others' requirements, thus morally defining the relationship boundaries.

To turn to the purpose of this paper, the impact of interpersonal touch in HRI has been investigated recently with a conclusion that touching intimate areas of a robots' body could trigger a physiological reaction [7]. This was a study conducted using 10 participants who interacted with a human shaped robot by touching the robot's less inaccessible areas of body. This particular approach, where we discern certain gaps, which we will explain when we present our three-phased study, instigated us to further investigate the conclusion and methodology.

This paper is presenting a pilot study conducted on the first phase of three phases study, where both male and female perception of robots and intimacies with robots are discussed. Our sample is limited to 32 individuals of both genders, who provided binary answers to questions that measured their perception to various aspects of human-robot interactions.

1.2 Objectives

As briefly mentioned above, this study is a pilot study of a part of a series of studies intending to be conducted on the topic of love and sex with robots. The series of studies are proposing to determine female perception and physiological responses to intimacy with robots. This pilot study, using both genders, is assessing the method that will be employed in the first stage of the series. The series, that we are proposing, will commence with a quantitative study of the perception of robots and intimacies with robots. At the second level, the physiological responses will be measured, and as the third level, a qualitative study will be conducted to understand the phenomenon.

In this paper, we are presenting the pilot study which we conducted using both genders, as a way of assessing the methodology. Our objective is not only to assess the method, but also to glean some insight into the perceptions of a group of individuals, of both gender, on human-robot interactions.

2 Methodology

2.1 Participants and Process

As indicated, this is an adaptation of a series of studies we are aiming to conduct on the subject of love and sex with robots. In this paper, there is an attempt to understand both male and female perception of robots and intimacy with robots. The focal point of this study is that, our objectives have not defined the representations of robots, either as a tool or a social agent. Our objective is for the participants to create scenarios with their insights and logic, and express their perception of representations, which we have not influenced; instead encouraged through numerous questions that stimulated scenarios both personal and impersonal. The next level of objective is to understand the attitudinal positioning of all participants as an aggregate on certain key criteria.

We have used the Guttman scaling method which is "…applied to a set of binary questions answered by a set of subjects" [8]. Guttman scale is cumulative, thus the questionnaire is progressively difficult, and the process could end with a wrong answer. In addition, Guttman requires binary answers to large number of questions. The justification for using this method is that it allows to understand the level of attitude towards the topic in discussion and the hierarchical structuring of the questionnaire helped to determine the ranking of the score and scale. Since our study is trying to understand the perception of robots in general and intimacy with robots, an attitudinal position as an aggregate, we maintain that this method adequately provided us the answers.

Most of our study participants are from our research institute, while others were selected using the referral sampling method used in non-probability technique. Thus, our participants are aged above 18 years, with varied education levels, and represent several nations. 32 participants, equally represented by gender, answered questions to 13 dimensions. These dimensions are derived from categories that examine particular aspects of the topic in question. The discussion of the results will build a conversation based on these aspects.

2.2 Results

From a 15 dimensions' questionnaire, only 13 dimensions were selected, omitting 2, thus deriving a valid Guttman Scale. A valid scale is which consisted of least errors, since large number of errors conveys the inability to reproduce a pattern of responses [9]. Guttman introduced the coefficient of reproducibility measure to as a measure of validity of the method [10]. Table 1 provides an overview of the study, the initial criteria, the dimensions built on each criterion, both positive and negative answers, detected errors and coefficient of reproducibility (CR) which required to be above 0.9 to have a valid scale.

Table 1. Overview of the study

Criteria	Dimensions	Positive	Negative	Errors	Coefficient of reproducibility (CR)
Awareness	2	338	110	32	0.92
Association	2	189	95	14	0.95
Enjoyment	2	109	243	11	0.96
Attraction	3	192	128	18	0.96
Intimacy	4	468	1132	72	0.95

3 Discussion

As mentioned before, this is part of a series of studies on intimacy with robots. Both male and female participated in this study, where they gave binary answers to succession of questions. This study is, by no means, attempting to establish a broad position on individuals' perspectives of robots, and intimacies with robots, but an attempt to establish an elementary level of understanding of the sample position in relation to the topic. This adaptation is an effort to build a conversation on challenges the topic is facing, and to open doors to further discussions.

The discussion will focus on introducing five criteria on which the study was based, and empirical analysis of results gained through the study.

3.1 Awareness

This criterion is primarily trying to comprehend the level of awareness of robots in the day to day living environments and the level of acceptability of that awareness. Here the awareness is separated in to two categories; awareness of robots in the living space and awareness of the human connection with robots. 80% of participants gave positive answers to this criterion, which contained two dimensions with 13 questions altogether. On the awareness of sharing living space in any capacity they envisage, perspectives of participants inclined towards positive (87.5%). Questions pertaining to the connections between humans and robots, starting with abstract level connections, and progressing to personal connections, majority (77%) tended to be positive. The objective of this dimension is to understand awareness of human-robot connections in various real-imagined scenarios, and the acceptability of both real and imagined possibilities for connections.

On the first dimension, participants naturally understood and accepted that robots are ubiquitous. The questions primarily inquired to the awareness of robots in their environment, from country, state to their workplace. However, in the second dimension where they answered 9 items, they gradually distance themselves from possible connections to the robots. Such as when asked whether they are aware that humans can have robots companions, majority of them accepted the possibility, however, when the same question was asked on a personal note, whether they are aware they can have robot companions, the majority answered negatively to the possibility.

In the awareness criteria, it is understood that awareness of the pervasiveness of robots has not created a further awareness of other promises of robots, such as in the roles of friends, or companions.

3.2 Association

Association is attempting to understand the kind of personal relations individuals prefer to build or imagines preferring to build, and the level of association they conceive they would prefer. Association is realized by asking questions from abstract to personal level such as whether preferring robots in the country perceived as positive as preferring to robots in home. At the second level trying to determine the perception of the preference to certain intimate connections with robots. Overall, 64% of participants answered positively to this criterion.

The first dimension where, the questions gradually progressed from abstract to personal level, 72% of participants gave positive answers, earlier questions garnering more positivity than latter. Question such as whether the participants prefer robots in their country elicits an overwhelming 93% of positivity while whether the participants like robots gaining nods of 56%. The second dimension brought participant to imagine close associations with robots, to which 49% gave positive answers. When asked whether the participants prefer being close with robots, their perspective turns negative only 37% answering positive.

On the criteria of association, associations are placed on a robot that is an abstract entity, that is relatively beyond the existing environs.

3.3 Enjoyment

Enjoyment is a criterion that is attempting to understand the individuals' pleasure and entrainment with/from robots. The objective is to introduce a robot as a pleasurable and entraining entity, and understand the accompanying perception. 55% percent of participants answered positively to ten questions on two dimensions. The first dimension is establishing whether robots are understood objectively as enjoyable and entertaining i.e. the perception that if robots are capable of creating and providing joy, then they are enjoyable. The second dimension is establishing a subjective position i.e. robots are enjoyable to me, and I can enjoy robots.

The first dimension drew 61% of positive answers, positions changing negative progressively at the end of six questions. Questions such as robots are enjoyable is a position that revealed favourable with 84% of participants agreeing with the statement, but robots themselves can be joyful did not elicit similar favorability, only 37% answering positively. The second dimension has an overall percentage of 51 positive answers. Questions such as robots provide joy is observed favourably with 59% of agreeable answers, while to a question that inquired whether robots are part of the joy is favored by 37% positivity.

It is noticeable from the answers that robots are considered as creators and providers of enjoyment, thus enjoyable, however there is a certain lack of enthusiasm to consider robots themselves as part of the process of enjoyment. Even though this perspective could sound overstated, the participants shows certain reluctance to share enjoyment with robots, considering robots as tools of entrainment.

3.4 Attraction

The objective of this criteria is to understand the perception of emotional attraction of individuals to robots. 28% of participants answered favorably to three scopes of the criteria. The objective of the first dimension is to establish the level of attraction at an abstract level with questions like 'do you find robots attractive?'. On the second level, the questions explored the possibility of being attracted to robots, making the perception personal to a certain extent. The third dimension expanded to directly establish attraction at a closely personal level, contesting the '...robots attractive' to establish '... attracted to robots'.

On the first scope, 44% answers elicit positivity, of which the question trying to ascertain the attractiveness of robots scored 56% of preference while whether that attractiveness could lead to emotional closeness is positively accepted by 34%. The second dimension received 24% positive answers, and to questions attempting to understand the possibility of an individual being emotionally close to a robot elicit 46% of favorability; however, to the question whether the emotional attraction is a possibility on a personal level gained 9% of positive answers. On the third dimension, with only 21% of positive answers, to the questions of whether participants, in any imagined scenario, be attracted emotionally to a robot gained a 9% favorable rate.

The responses to this criterion revealed that some participants find robots attractive, and perceived that individuals could be emotionally attracted to robots. However, on the personal level, the possibility of being emotionally attracted to a robot, majority of participants found implausible. Thus, the higher majority of participants revealed a clear case of acceptance to certain hypothetical scenarios with robots, but with the attitude of 'not me', declining to put themselves in the scenario.

3.5 Intimacy

The objective of this criteria is to understand the perception of intimacy, hypothetically conjured, with robots. The questions on this category started from abstract level gradually progressing to personal positions. 25% of participants positively responded to four dimensions where they answered altogether 50 questions. On the first dimensions the questions were attempting to understand the perception of an intimate relationship with robots; starting from outlying level. i.e. perception of humans in an intimate relationship with robot, towards personal level i.e. the participant in an intimate relationship with robots. 28% participants answered favorably to this criterion. The second dimension was intended to ascertain the perception of love with robots, where questions were arranged in the similar manner to the dimension one. 35% of participants answered positively to 12 questions. The third dimension introduced the sensual involvement, attempting to understand the perception of sensual feelings related to robots. Overall 23% of participants provided positive answers. The fourth dimension gathered only 15% of positive answered from participants who answered 14 questions. The scope of this section is understanding the perception of sex with robots. The questions were organized in the same manner as previous three dimensions; gradually progressing from abstract level questions to personal level.

On the first dimension, when questioned on the possibility of humans having intimate relationships with robots 56% answered positively, however, when presented with the question whether the participants personally associate intimately with robots 15% participants positively answered. The possibility of humans loving robots, 59% of participants considered as positive, however, when it reached the personal level, 28% of participants gave positive answers. The third dimension where the first question is whether there is a possibility of a sensual involvement between humans and robots, 43% accepted the possibility, and only 12.5% participants gave positive answers to a personal sensual involvement. Sex with a robot is the least favored with only 31% agreeing to the possibility of sex between humans and robots. Only 9% wanted to imagine personal sexual involvement with a robot.

On this criterion, the dimensions developed from emotional to physical involvement with robots, and it was evident that emotional involvement is slightly favored over physical involvement.

As discussed before, and as can be seen in Figs. 1 and 2, in general, abstract emotional and physical level is acceptable to majority of the participants, but the personal involvements are mostly perceived as negative. Throughout this analysis, participants distanced themselves from the perception of being intimately involved with robots, creating a 'self and other' and 'over there but not here' distinction. This distinction could be an adoption of a moral position, not simply with regards to love and sex with robots, which is a highly-contested topic, but also corresponding to human-robot interactions in general. Naturally, there are numerous aspects to human perceptions of relationships, even human-human relationships, and number of elements that compels them. Culture, and economy perform major roles in shaping everyday living of humans, impacting their

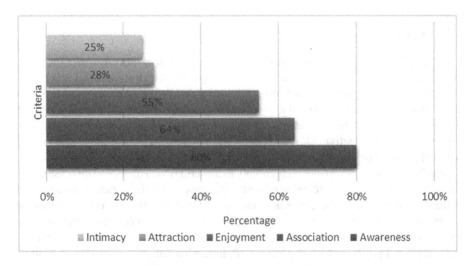

Fig. 1. Overview of overall positive answers

perceptions of morality in relationships. Those factors have not played a role in this study, which could be considered as a limitation. However, we intend to remedy that omission in the third phase of the proposed series of studies.

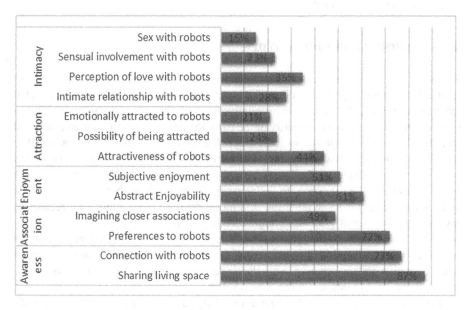

Fig. 2. Overview of the percentage of positive answers to each criterion

3.6 Limitations of the Study

Although this is a pilot study, there are several limitations that required mentioning at this stage. The first limitation is the method of inquiry, which we would like to state is not adequate. Quantitative analysis of hypothetical positions adopted by individuals is commonly performed. However, in this study, examining the answers, considering the binary options provided for answering, and unofficial discussions with some of the participants, we have come to the realization that, for a comprehensive study, adopting both qualitative and quantitative will resulted in rich outcomes.

The subject matter itself presented limitation, considering that human-robot inter-actions are still at the progressing stage, and even though scholars are predicting and painting highly interactive human-robot environments, at this point in time, love and sex with robots is a hypothetical future. Thus, participants of this study need to imagine scenarios and associate to them, or relate to cultural- moral norms, or simply based their answers on justice and fairness.

On the other hand, we did not define the parameters for robots, giving the freedom for participants to imagine for themselves. The advantage in this approach is that it has broaden the representation of robots, thus expanding the imagination. However, on certain criteria, like enjoyment, the robots inclined to be considered as just toys or in intimacies as sex toys.

The binary answering option this study recommended is understood as a limitation, considering that yes or no will not adequately compensate for numerous nuances some of the questions presented. We endeavored to counterbalance this issue through an empirical discussion of results.

4 Conclusion and Future Work

This study has attempted to comprehend the perception of human-robot interactions, in terms of how humans perceive robots and intimacies with robots. Our sample revealed that their awareness of robots as positive, however, majority is negative to the possibility of being attracted to a robot. Majority of the participants reacted positively to emotional and physical bonding with robots in abstract, distant level, an attitude they adopted to all queries. However, on a personal level of interaction with robots, majority responded negatively. It is noted that participants created a 'self and other' and 'over there but not here' distinction when it comes to their perception of human-robot relationship. The authors recognize this as an adoption of a moral position, not simply with regards to love and sex with robots, but also communicating to HRI.

As we have been mentioning throughout this paper, we are aiming to conduct a series of studies on the perception of human-computer interaction. We will conduct studies of both qualitative and quantitative methods to understand the perception and also a physiological response to intimately touching a robot.

Perceptions of human-robot interactions (HRI) have a certain impact on how individuals comprehend intimacies with robots. Perceptions are products of awareness and logical reasoning, which is not to say that one correlates with the other or both are there at the same time. Unless there is an extensive conversation on topics of HRI, informed reasoning and creation will take a backbench to wild, and ill-informed conceptions and creations. On the other hand, HRI needs these dialogues to assist in their creative ventures, not just to imagine how emotions and desires should feature in the cognition of a robot, but also to imagine the 'freedom to think' and what it could mean to humans-robot relationship.

References

1. Levy, D.: Love and Sex with Robots. Harper Collins, New York (2009)
2. Asimov, I.: Runaround. Astounding Sci. Fiction **29**(1), 94–103 (1942)
3. Coeckelbergh, M.: Moral appearances: emotions, robots, and human morality. Ethics Inf. Technol. **12**(3), 235–241 (2010)
4. Piçarra, N., et al.: Making sense of social robots: a structural analysis of the layperson's social representation of robots. Revue Européenne de Psychologie Appliquée/Eur. Rev. Appl. Psychol. **66**(6), 277–289 (2016)
5. Kim, M.-S., Kim, E.-J.: Humanoid robots as "The Cultural Other": are we able to love our creations? AI Soc. **28**(3), 309–318 (2013)
6. Scheutz, M., Arnold, T.: Are we ready for sex robots? In: The Eleventh ACM/IEEE International Conference on Human Robot Interation. IEEE Press (2016)

7. Li, J., Ju, W., Reeves, B.: Touching a mechanical body: tactile contact with intimate parts of a humanoid robot is physiologically arousing. In: 66th Annual Conference of the International Communication Association. Fukuoka, Japan (2016)

8. Abdi, H.: Guttman scaling. Encyclopedia of Research Design. SAGE Publications, Thousand Oaks (2010)

9. Alvarelhão, J., Lopes, D.: A guttman scale to assess knowledge about sexually transmitted diseases in adults with cerebral palsy. Sex. Disabil. **34**(4), 485–493 (2016)

10. Bailey, K.: Methods of social research. Simon and Schuster (2008)

Author Index

Printed in the United States
By Bookmasters